UNDERSTANDING

TEMPLE SYMBOLS

THROUGH **SCRIPTURE**, **HISTORY**, AND **ART**

UNDERSTANDING

TEMPLE SYMBOLS

THROUGH **SCRIPTURE**,
HISTORY, AND **ART**

JACK M. LYON

DESERET
BOOK

Salt Lake City, Utah

More information related to this book may be found at http://www.templethoughts.com

Library of Congress Cataloging-in-Publication Data

Names: Lyon, Jack M., author.
Title: Understanding temple symbols through scripture, history, and art / Jack M. Lyon.
Description: Salt Lake City, Utah : Deseret Book, [2016] | Includes bibliographical references and index.
Identifiers: LCCN 2016026984 | ISBN 9781629722443 (hardbound : alk. paper)
Subjects: LCSH: Mormon temples. | Temple work (Mormon Church) | The Church of Jesus Christ of Latter-day Saints—Doctrines. | Mormon Church—Doctrines.
Classification: LCC BX8643.T4 L96 2016 | DDC 246/.95893—dc23
LC record available at https://lccn.loc.gov/2016026984

Printed in China
Four Colour Print Group, Nansha, China

10   9   8   7   6   5   4   3   2   1

We live in a world of symbols.
No man or woman can come out of the temple
endowed as he should be, unless he has seen,
beyond the symbol, the mighty realities
for which the symbols stand.

ELDER JOHN A. WIDTSOE

Woodblock print from Camille Flammarion's 1888 book L'atmosphère: météorologie populaire.

The Queen of Sheba before the Temple of Solomon in Jerusalem, *detail, by Salomon de Bray. Oil on panel, 1657.*

CONTENTS

HOLINESS
to the
LORD.
THE
HOUSE of the
LORD
BUILT BY THE
CHURCH
of
JESUS CHRIST
of
LATTER-DAY
SAINTS,
COMMENCED
APRIL 6. 1853
COMPLETED
APRIL 6. 1893.

Gilded engraving on the central east tower of the Salt Lake Temple.

THINKING ABOUT THE TEMPLE

Perhaps after finishing a temple session, you have sat quietly in the celestial room, thinking about what you have just experienced. The elegant furnishings, the soaring windows, the sparkling chandeliers, all join to lift the mind from earth to heaven. In the silence of those sacred precincts, we can leave the world behind and ponder the things of eternity. As Joseph Smith said, "The things of God are of deep import; and time, and experience, and careful and ponderous and solemn thoughts can only find them out."[1]

The purpose of this book is to help us think about the temple experience more deeply, so that we better understand the nature of God and his eternal purposes for his children: "This is my work and my glory—to bring to pass the immortality and eternal life of man" (Moses 1:39).

We sometimes think that we cannot discuss the endowment *at all* outside the temple, but that is not so, for parts of it have been commented upon and even quoted in general conference and in Church publications; some things are discussed on the Church's website at LDS.org. Nevertheless, certain sacred matters should be kept strictly within the walls of the temple, and here we will discuss only what is mentioned in the scriptures, in official Church publications, or in Church-sanctioned publications, focusing on possible connections between the temple, the scriptures,[2] and various works of art for the edification of those who have "eyes to see" and "ears to hear" (Ezekiel 12:2).

---

1. http://josephsmithpapers.org, History, 1838–1856, volume C-1 [2 November 1838–31 July 1842], 904[b].
2. Italics in quotations have been added for emphasis throughout.

Adoration of the Magi, *by Fra Angelico and*
Fra Filippo Lippi. Tempera on poplar panel, about 1450.

THE FORGOTTEN WORLD OF SYMBOLS

Hanging in a prominent spot in the National Gallery in Washington, D.C., is a painting by two Catholic monks, Fra Angelico ("Brother Angel") and Fra Filippo Lippi. Known as *Adoration of the Magi,* the painting is large, just a little more than fifty-four inches in diameter, and is a stunning thing to see; its colors, already rich and vibrant, are accented with burnished gold. The work was finished in about the year 1460, during an era when most people were intensely religious but could not read, even if books had been available to them. (The printing press was a new invention; Gutenberg published his famous Bible in 1455.) But people could—and did—go to church, where they encountered a profusion of scriptural knowledge, illustrated with symbols and expressed in glorious paintings and luminous stained glass. They could not read letters, but they *could* read pictures, and they did so very well, in ways that have been almost forgotten by us.

Look closely at the painting, as there is much to see.[3] On the lower right, near the center, is the Christ-child, his hand raised in a symbolic gesture still used by Catholics today—the sign of blessing.[4] (The two raised fingers and thumb represent the Trinity.) Worshiping before the Christ-child are the three kings, each wearing a diadem of gold. One king, dressed in red, is placing his hand over his heart, pledging allegiance to his heavenly King. Another, in blue, indicates his unconditional faithfulness. The third king reverently touches the Savior's heel, which will someday crush the serpent's head (see Genesis 3:14–15 and footnotes).

Standing near the stable, in plain, ragged clothing, are two of the shepherds who were "abiding in the field, keeping watch over their flock by night" (Luke 2:8). One is pointing at the manger, where the angel had said

---

3. See image details, pages 3–5. Readers who want to examine the painting in greater detail can do so online: http://www.nga.gov/content/ngaweb/Collection/art-object-page.41581.html.

4. What appears to be the Christ-child's rattle is actually a pomegranate, whose many seeds represent the heirs of salvation (see Isaiah 53:10; Mosiah 15:10).

they would find "the babe wrapped in swaddling clothes" (Luke 2:12). The other is raising his hands in wonder and adoration. This posture can also be seen as a sign of prayer: "Hear the voice of my supplications, when I cry unto thee, when I lift up my hands toward thy holy oracle" (Psalm 28:2). Praying with uplifted hands was standard practice in New Testament times; for example, the apostle Paul wrote, "I will . . . that men pray every where, lifting up holy hands, without wrath and doubting" (1 Timothy 2:8). On the right of the painting, standing near Joseph, is a third shepherd. Raising his right hand, he swears to be true to the Savior. A hole in his clothing exposes his knee, reminding us that "at the name of Jesus every knee should bow" (Philippians 2:10).

The peacock, perched on a beam of the stable, suggests the Resurrection, as its flesh was thought to be incorruptible; its beautiful plumage represents the glory of God. The stable itself is plain but solidly built, standing on a sure foundation, while the great and spacious buildings behind it, symbolizing "the kingdoms of this world," are broken and crumbling, their dominion reduced to rubble. "Babylon the great is fallen" (Revelation 11:15; 18:2).

Coming to worship, as Lehi saw in vision, are "numberless concourses of people, . . . pressing forward, that they might obtain . . . the love of God" (1 Nephi 8:21; 11:25). These people are enclosed in a great circle, which represents eternity. From alpha to omega, from beginning to end, the advent of the Savior is the central fact of human existence, historically and for each of us individually. As a well-known Christmas carol says, "Where meek souls will receive him / *Still* the dear Christ enters in."

Much more could be said about the symbols in this painting. For example, the dog featured prominently at the bottom of the scene is a symbol of loyalty and fidelity. (Even today, some dogs are named "Fido," which is the Latin word for "faithful.") Thus, the dog reminds us that we should be faithful to our Master, who has now come into the world.

Many other such works of art, most of which were created in medieval or Renaissance times and are generally unfamiliar to Latter-day Saints, are included here. Because of their religious symbolism, we can learn much from these beautiful creations to help us understand the meaning of what we see in the temple, which is also rich in religious symbolism.

For the most part, we who live in the modern world are unfamiliar with the symbolic worldview that our ancestors understood and treasured. Instead, we value what is literal and real. But there is also great worth in the more symbolic artwork produced in the past. It may not be realistic, but the meaning *behind* the symbols (for example, angels with wings) is very real indeed.[5] It is from that more symbolic, nearly forgotten point of view that this book proceeds.

---

5. Joseph Smith explained that "wings are a representation of power, to move, to act, etc." (D&C 77:4).

Understanding the meaning of the temple is a lifetime endeavor based on our individual needs, faith, and effort, and on the Lord's wisdom and will. For each of us, such understanding is incomplete and thus can only be touched on here (see suggested reading list, p. 147). But perhaps the things we discuss here can help us think more deeply about our temple experiences and find the greater light and knowledge promised to those who seek it:

Ask,

AND IT SHALL BE GIVEN YOU;

SEEK,

AND YE SHALL FIND;

knock,

AND IT SHALL BE OPENED UNTO YOU.

(MATTHEW 7:7)

Salt Lake Temple, detail of west side doors.

TEMPLE SYMBOLS

Elder John A. Widtsoe served as an apostle from 1921 until his death in 1952. Deeply involved with temple and genealogy work, he wrote, "No man or woman can come out of the temple endowed as he should be, unless he has seen, beyond the symbols, the mighty realities for which the symbols stand" ("Temple Worship," 62).

"But why," many people wonder, "must we use symbols? Why can't the temple ceremony just tell us plainly what we need to know?" The problem is that some things *cannot* be explained in plainness. How, for example, could you *tell* someone how to ride a bicycle? The only way to learn is to do it, to have the actual experience. Many things in life are like that, including life itself.

The Prophet Joseph Smith said, "Reading the experience of others, or the revelation given to them, can never give us a comprehensive view of our condition and true relation to God. Knowledge of these things can only be obtained by experience through the ordinances of God set forth for that purpose."[1]

Elder Boyd K. Packer explained, "If you will go to the temple and *remember that the teaching is symbolic,* you will never go in the proper spirit without coming away with your vision extended, feeling a little more exalted, with your knowledge increased as to things that are spiritual" ("The Holy Temple," 34).

There are several keys that can help us understand these sacred symbols.

---

1. http://josephsmithpapers.org, History, 1838–1856, volume E-1 [1 July 1843–30 April 1844], 1750.

KEY 1: A SYMBOL RESEMBLES THE THING IT STANDS FOR

One key to understanding a symbol is that it often resembles the thing it stands for. For example, the bread and water of the sacrament represent the body and blood of the Savior—in that order. It would make no sense to have bread represent the Savior's blood or to have water represent the Savior's body. Bread, like flesh, is solid; water, like blood, is liquid.

Another example is the decoration embroidered on the clothing of the high priest in the Old Testament: "They made upon the hems of the [high priest's] robe pomegranates of blue, and purple, and scarlet" (Exodus 39:24). Have you ever eaten a pomegranate? If so, you know that it is full of seeds. So the pomegranate can be seen as a symbol of fertility, of posterity. In addition, the juice of the pomegranate is red, suggesting blood, or life: "The life of all flesh is the blood thereof" (Leviticus 17:14).

After Adam and Eve partook of the forbidden fruit, "they knew that they were naked; and they sewed fig leaves together, and made themselves aprons" (Genesis 3:7). What color are fig leaves? Green, which symbolizes life and growth. Figs also contain hundreds of tiny seeds, so the fig, like the pomegranate, can represent fertility and posterity. In addition, it was only after the Fall that Adam and Eve were able to have children. As Eve said, "Were it not for our transgression we never should have had seed" (Moses 5:9–11).

KEY 2: SYMBOLS CAN HAVE MORE THAN ONE MEANING

Just because a symbol represents one thing doesn't mean it cannot represent another as well. For example, the "seed" that Eve mentioned (her posterity) also has another meaning: "The Lord God said unto the serpent, . . . I will put enmity between thee and the woman, and between thy seed and her seed; it shall bruise thy head, and thou shalt bruise his heel" (Genesis 3:14–15). The footnote in the Latter-day Saint edition of the Bible points out that the word translated here as "it" is really "he" in Hebrew: "*he* shall bruise thy head." In addition, the footnotes explain, the Hebrew word translated as "bruise" can also mean "crush, or grind": "he shall crush thy head." Finally, in the original Hebrew, the word for "seed" is singular rather than plural; this verse refers to one *specific* "seed," the Savior. Hebrews 2:14 explains, "As the children are partakers of flesh and blood,

This depiction of the Crucifixion, a stained-glass window from Chartres Cathedral, shows the Savior on a cross of green and red, the colors of life, prefiguring his and our resurrection. In the Middle Ages, the cross was thought to have been made of wood from the tree of life.

[Jesus] . . . himself . . . took part of the same; that through death he might destroy him that had the power of death, that is, the devil."

Again consider the sacrament. Yes, the bread and water represent the Savior's body and blood. But they also, in themselves, provide nourishment. Thus, they represent both death *and* life, showing that Jesus died so we might live. Baptism has these same two meanings. We go down into the water, which represents death, and we come up out of the water, which represents a new birth, both physical and spiritual: "We are buried with [Christ] by baptism into death: that like as Christ was raised up from the dead by the glory of the Father, even so we also should walk in newness of life. For if we have been planted together in the likeness of his death, we shall be also in the likeness of his resurrection" (Romans 6:3–5).

KEY 3: SYMBOLS CAN HAVE SUGGESTED MEANINGS
AS WELL AS SPECIFIC MEANINGS

Symbols with specific meanings (such as the bread and water of the sacrament) can also *suggest* other meanings. In other words, they have connotations as well as denotations. For example, bread (as used in the sacrament) tastes good. That fact may bring to mind Alma's sermon on planting the Lord's word in our hearts: "If ye do not cast it out by your unbelief, that ye will resist the Spirit of the Lord, behold, it will begin to swell within your breasts; and when you feel these swelling motions, ye will begin to say within yourselves—It must needs be that this is a good seed, or that the word is good, for it beginneth to enlarge my soul; yea, it beginneth to enlighten my understanding, yea, *it beginneth to be delicious to me*" (Alma 32:28).

The refreshing water used in the sacrament may make us think about the Savior's words to the woman at the well: "Whosoever drinketh of the water that I shall give him shall never thirst; but the water that I shall give him shall be in him a well of water springing up into everlasting life" (John 4:14).

Alma's conclusion may apply to the sacrament as a whole: "Ye shall feast upon this fruit even until ye are filled, *that ye hunger not, neither shall ye thirst*" (Alma 32:42).

KEY 4: WE CAN UNDERSTAND SYMBOLS
BY COMPARING THEM WITH OTHER SYMBOLS

Sometimes we can understand a symbol better by comparing it with another symbol. This is true in the scriptures as well as in the temple. For example, consider the differences in the sacrament prayers:

O God, the Eternal Father, we ask thee in the name of thy Son, Jesus Christ, to bless and sanctify this bread to the souls of all those who partake of it,[2] that they may eat in remembrance of the body of thy Son, and witness unto thee, O God, the Eternal Father, that they are willing to take upon them the name of thy Son, and always remember him and keep his commandments which he has given them; that they may always have his Spirit to be with them. Amen. [D&C 20:77]

———————————

2. The sacrament provides constant nourishment to the soul, which comprises both body and spirit (see D&C 88:15).

O God, the Eternal Father, we ask thee in the name of thy Son, Jesus Christ, to bless and sanctify this wine to the souls of all those who drink of it, that they may do it in remembrance of the blood of thy Son, which was shed for them; that they may witness unto thee, O God, the Eternal Father, that they do always remember him, that they may have his Spirit to be with them. Amen. [D&C 20:79]

When we take the bread, we witness to God that we are *willing* to do certain things. When we take the water, we witness to God that we *do* just one of those things. Why might that be?

Here is another example: In the book of Abraham, the Gods create the earth; then they create animals in the following way:

The Gods organized the earth to bring forth the beasts after their kind, and cattle after their kind, and every thing that creepeth upon the earth after its kind; and the Gods saw they would obey. [Abraham 4:25]

In this account, the Gods, still in heaven, organize the earth to bring forth the animals. But when the time comes to create man, the Gods use a different method:

The Gods took counsel among themselves and said: Let us go down and form man in our image, after our likeness. . . . [And] the Gods went down to organize man in their own image, in the image of the Gods to form they him, male and female to form they them. [Abraham 4:26–27]

What can we learn from noticing the *differences* in those two methods of creation? As Joseph Smith taught, "By proving contraries, truth is made manifest" (*History of the Church,* 6:248).

KEY 5: SYMBOLS CAN BUILD UPON OTHER SYMBOLS

In the two west corner towers of the Manti Utah Temple are beautiful freestanding spiral staircases, built without central supports. These are a marvel of engineering and pioneer construction, with each step supporting the step above it as the stairs rise five stories to the temple's upper level. These spiral stairs are also wonderful symbols of growth and progression, bringing to mind these words from the Prophet Joseph Smith:

When you climb up a ladder, you must begin at the bottom, and ascend step by step, until you arrive at the top; and so it is with the principles of the gospel—you must begin with the first,

Nauvoo Temple spiral staircase, by William Weeks.
Original architectural drawing, 1840.

and go on until you learn all the principles of exaltation. But it will be a great while after you have passed through the veil before you will have learned them. It is not all to be comprehended in this world; it will be a great work to learn our salvation and exaltation even beyond the grave. [*Joseph Smith,* 268]

The spiral stairs also bring to mind this story from the Old Testament:

Jacob went out from Beer-sheba, . . . and he lighted upon a certain place, and tarried there all night. . . . And he dreamed, and behold a ladder set up on the earth, and the top of it reached to heaven: and behold the angels of God ascending and descending on it.

And, behold, the Lord stood above it, and said, I am the Lord God of Abraham thy father, and the God of Isaac: the land whereon thou liest, to thee will I give it, and to thy seed; and thy seed shall be as the dust of the earth, . . . and in thy seed shall all the families of the earth be blessed. . . .

And Jacob awaked out of his sleep, and he said, Surely the Lord is in this place. . . . This is none other but the house of God, and this is the gate of heaven. [Genesis 28:10–17]

Jacob's Dream, by William Blake. Pen and gray ink and watercolor, about 1800.

Like Jacob's ladder leading to heaven, the temple staircases illustrate the idea that one symbol can build upon another, leading us upward in our understanding. This idea is also symbolized by the floor levels in some of the temples. For example, in both the Salt Lake and the Manti temples, participants do not just go from room to room but move physically *upward* as they go. The creation room leads upward to the garden room, the garden room leads upward to the world room, and so on, until they reach the celestial room. In temples where participants do not move from room to room, the same concept is symbolized by increasing the brightness of the lights as the endowment progresses.

The concept of upward progression is also taught in the covenants we make during the endowment. Little children, for example, need to learn *obedience* to their parents. Young and inexperienced, they must constantly be told what to do—and what not to do. When parents say, "Don't play in the street," a child's disobedience can mean injury or even death. As children grow older, however, they learn to do things from a sense of duty. For example, they might not want to pay tithing, but they make that *sacrifice* because they understand it as a law they should follow. Later, after coming to more fully understand the *gospel,* they might pay tithing out of love for the Lord. But as spiritually mature adults, the same people will pay tithing as a matter of *consecration,* because their hearts' desire is to build the kingdom of God and establish the cause of Zion. At that point, they have internalized the principles of the gospel, and their purposes are the same as God's.

These concepts are true regarding individual progression, and the same principle applies in the collective history of God's people through the ages. The Pearl of Great Price tells us:

> Adam and Eve, his wife, called upon the name of the Lord. . . . And he gave unto them commandments, that they should worship the Lord their God, and should offer the firstlings of their flocks, for an offering unto the Lord. And Adam was obedient unto the commandments of the Lord.
>
> And after many days an angel of the Lord appeared unto Adam, saying: Why dost thou offer sacrifices unto the Lord? And Adam said unto him: I know not, save the Lord commanded me. [Moses 5:4–6]

Adam didn't understand the reason for offering sacrifice: he did it from obedience, because the Lord had commanded him to do so. Then the angel explained its meaning: "This thing is a similitude of the sacrifice of the Only Begotten of the Father, which is full of grace and truth" (Moses 5:7).

From then on, God's people kept the law of sacrifice as practiced by the patriarchs and then under the law of Moses: "Ye shall bring your burnt offerings, and your sacrifices, and your tithes, and heave offerings of your hand, and your vows, and your freewill offerings, and the firstlings of your herds and of your flocks" (Deuteronomy 12:6).

The law of sacrifice continued until the death of the Savior, who was the "great and last sacrifice; . . . yea, infinite and eternal" (Alma 34:14). Thus, the law of sacrifice was fulfilled by the law of the gospel. As Paul wrote, "The [sacrificial] law [of Moses] was our schoolmaster to bring us unto Christ, that we might be justified by faith. But after that faith is come, we are no longer under a schoolmaster. For ye are all the children of God by faith in Christ Jesus" (Galatians 3:24–26).

Today, we continue to live the law of the gospel. But the day will come when we live the law of consecration, not because it is required of us but because our own overriding purpose in life is to build the kingdom of God: "This is Zion—the pure in heart" (D&C 97:21).

Many other symbols in the temple build upon one another, teaching the principle of progression. The endowment is not a horizontal journey; it is a symbolic *ascension* to the heavenly realms.

KEY 6: SYMBOLS CAN MEAN DIFFERENT THINGS IN DIFFERENT CIRCUMSTANCES AND TO DIFFERENT PEOPLE

The temple is a place of revelation, and sometimes the Lord uses its symbols to bless us with the knowledge we need *as individuals* to solve specific problems in our lives. Elder John A. Widtsoe wrote:

> In temple worship, as in all else, we probably gain understanding according to our differing knowledge and capacity; but I believe that we can increase in knowledge and enlarge our capacity, and in that way receive greater gifts from God. I would therefore urge upon you that we teach those who go into the temples to do so with a strong desire to have God's will revealed to them, for comfort, peace, and success in our daily lives, not for publication, or for conversation, but for our own good, for the satisfying of our hearts. ["Temple Worship," 64]

Elder Widtsoe was not speaking about revelation only on spiritual matters; he saw it in very practical terms:

> I believe that the busy person on the farm, in the shop, in the office, or in the household, who has his worries and troubles, can solve his problems better and more quickly in the house of the Lord than anywhere else. If he will leave his problems behind and in the temple work for himself

and for his dead, he will confer a mighty blessing upon those who have gone before, and quite as large a blessing will come to him, for at the most unexpected moments, in or out of the temple, will come to him, as a revelation, the solution of the problems that vex his life. That is the gift that comes to those who enter the temple properly, because it is a place where revelations may be expected. I bear my personal testimony that this is so. ["Temple Worship," 62]

Elder Widtsoe, who was a scientist, gave the following example from his own life:

For several years, under a Federal grant with my staff of workers, we had gathered thousands of data in the field of soil moisture; but I could not extract any general law running through them. I gave up at last. My wife and I went to the temple that day to forget the failure. In the third endowment room, out of the unseen, came the solution. [*In a Sunlit Land,* 177]

Elder Widtsoe summarized:

To the man or woman who goes through the temple, with open eyes, heeding the symbols and the covenants, and making a steady, continuous effort to understand the full meaning, God speaks His word, and revelations come. ["Temple Worship," 62]

KEY 7: SYMBOLS ARE DESIGNED TO RAISE QUESTIONS IN YOUR MIND

As you participate in the endowment, the presentation may raise questions in your mind. That is by *design,* as questions can lead us to answers and to greater knowledge. So acknowledge your questions and use them as a starting point for further thinking and study. President Dieter F. Uchtdorf explained:

We are a question-asking people because we know that inquiry leads to truth. That is the way the Church got its start—from a young man who had questions. In fact, I'm not sure how one can discover truth without asking questions. In the scriptures you will rarely discover a revelation that didn't come in response to a question. Whenever a question arose and Joseph Smith wasn't sure of the answer, he approached the Lord, and the results are the wonderful revelations in the Doctrine and Covenants. Often the knowledge Joseph received extended far beyond the original question. That is because not only can the Lord answer the questions we ask but, even more importantly, He can give us answers to questions we should have asked. Let us listen to those answers. . . .

God commands us to seek answers to our questions and asks only that we seek "with a sincere heart, with real intent, having faith in Christ." When we do so, the truth of all things can be manifested to us "by the power of the Holy Ghost." ["Reflection in the Water"]

Consider the depiction of Jesus' nativity in one of the stained-glass windows of the magnificent cathedral in Chartres, France. The glaziers who made the windows were teaching in a symbolic way, much as we do in the temple. Look closely at the manger holding the baby Jesus. Do you notice anything unusual about it? Does it raise a question in your mind?

If you pause to ponder, you might realize that the manger resembles an altar—and that is by design. The artists who created that window wanted us to understand that this child in the manger would be offered as a sacrifice for sin. As the book of Hebrews says, "Neither by the blood of goats and calves, but by *his own blood* he entered . . . into the holy place [in the temple], having obtained eternal redemption for

Nativity of Jesus. *Incarnation window, panel 3, Chartres Cathedral, between about 1205 and 1215.*

us" (Hebrews 9:12). As Amulek explained, "It is expedient that there should be a great and last sacrifice, . . . and that great and last sacrifice will be the Son of God, yea, infinite and eternal" (Alma 34:13–14).

Here is another example, this time a verse from the Pearl of Great Price describing conditions in the time of Adam and Eve: "The Gospel began to be preached, from the beginning, being declared by holy angels sent forth from the presence of God" (Moses 5:58).

That verse raises a question: Who were these angels? Latter-day Saint scholar Hugh Nibley gave one explanation: "The Mandaean literature will tell you that the messengers that came to instruct Adam and Eve were the apostles who later became the pillars of the Church (Peter, James, and John)" (*Ancient Documents and the Pearl of Great Price*, 3). It is possible to take Brother Nibley's statement at face value, for certainly the Lord later sent Peter, James, and John to Joseph Smith and Oliver Cowdery to restore the Melchizedek Priesthood. But his statement also raises *other* questions: "Why would Peter, James, and John visit Adam and Eve? Aren't they from a completely different time period? Did they come as premortal spirits? What is going on here?" Possibly these messengers were not literally Peter, James, and John but symbolically represent any true messengers "sent forth" to visit "Adam and Eve" (us) here in mortality. The very word *apostle,* in the original Greek (*apostolos*), means "one who is sent."

In the temple are a number of things we may have vaguely wondered about but haven't actually thought about or researched. But we should! The process is like finding a loose bit of yarn on an old sweater. It's easy to ignore that bit of yarn and just go on our way. But if we begin pulling on it, we may find it's the end of a very long strand with all kinds of interesting twists and turns.

KEY 8: TEMPLE SYMBOLS CAN BE EXPLORED THROUGH THE SCRIPTURES

S. Michael Wilcox, author of *House of Glory,* wrote:

> Occasionally I have been asked if I can recommend a good book or article to help people understand the temple ordinances. I have always answered, "Yes! There is a wonderful manual written to explain even the most subtle meanings of the endowment, and it is readily available to you." Excitedly the person takes out pencil and paper to write down the title. "The manual is the holy scriptures," I say. Disappointed, the person puts down the pencil and says, "No, really. Is there any other book you would recommend?" [Page 19]

Brother Wilcox knows what he is talking about. If we start looking at the scriptures with the temple in mind, we will begin to see the many parallels between the two, and these parallels can enhance our understanding, even when the scriptures at first glance might not *seem* to be about the temple. Here is an example in the Doctrine and Covenants, from a revelation to President

On the central west tower of the Salt Lake Temple is a bas-relief carving of Ursa Major, the Big Dipper. As any Boy Scout knows, an imaginary line running upward through the two outside stars of this constellation leads to Polaris, the North Star, around which, from the viewpoint of planet Earth, all the other stars appear to revolve. Thus, this carving, like a mariner's compass, is a symbol of direction, of finding our path through life. Interestingly, the stars in the carving are aligned so that they point to the actual North Star.

Brigham Young about how to organize the pioneer companies as they prepared to leave Winter Quarters and move west: "Let all the people of The Church of Jesus Christ of Latter-day Saints, and those who journey with them, be organized into companies, with a covenant and promise to keep all the commandments and statutes of the Lord our God" (D&C 136:2). This revelation was given as very practical instruction. And yet how many parallels with the temple are in that one short verse? And what can those parallels teach us? Aren't we, too, on a journey together to Zion?

Another example is found in the Book of Mormon in which Alma discusses the Liahona. It includes many parallels that can enhance our understanding of the endowment:

> And now, my son, I would that ye should understand that these things are not without a shadow; for as our fathers [Lehi and his family] were slothful to give heed to this compass (now these things were temporal) they did not prosper; even so it is with things which are spiritual. For behold, it is as easy to give heed to the word of Christ, which will point to you a straight course to eternal bliss, as it was for our fathers to give heed to this compass, which would point unto them a straight course to the promised land.
>
> And now I say, is there not a type in this thing? For just as surely as this director did bring our fathers, by following its course, to the promised land, shall the words of Christ, if we follow their course, carry us beyond this vale of sorrow into a far better land of promise. [Alma 37:43–45]

KEY 9: GOSPEL SYMBOLS TESTIFY OF THE SAVIOR AND HIS ATONEMENT

After Adam's baptism, the Lord explained to him its symbolism, noting, "All things are created and made to bear record of me, both things which are temporal, and things which are spiritual; things which are in the heavens above, and things which are on the earth, and things which are in the earth, and things which are under the earth, both above and beneath: all things bear record of me" (Moses 6:63).

Consider the parable of the good Samaritan:

> A certain man went down from Jerusalem to Jericho, and fell among thieves, which stripped him of his raiment, and wounded him, and departed, leaving him half dead.

The Good Samaritan Leading the Pilgrim to an Inn. *Creation and good Samaritan window, panel 10, Chartres Cathedral, between about 1205 and 1215.*

And by chance there came down a certain priest that way: and when he saw him, he passed by on the other side. And likewise a Levite, when he was at the place, came and looked on him, and passed by on the other side.

But a certain Samaritan, as he journeyed, came where he was: and when he saw him, he had compassion on him, and went to him, and bound up his wounds, pouring in oil and wine, and set him on his own beast, and brought him to an inn, and took care of him.

And on the morrow when he departed, he took out two pence, and gave them to the host, and said unto him, Take care of him; and whatsoever thou spendest more, when I come again, I will repay thee. [Luke 10:30–35]

We think about this parable as an admonition to help those in need, but perhaps it has another interpretation, as shown in another window from the cathedral at Chartres. In this scene, the good

Samaritan has picked up the wounded man, "set him on his own beast," and is now taking him to an inn. As you look at that picture, do you notice anything unusual about the good Samaritan? The good Samaritan looks like Jesus. In fact, he *is* Jesus.

Why would that be so? What were the unknown artists who made this window telling us? Could it be that *we* are the wounded man and that it is the Savior who rescues us from our precarious condition? What does the parable tell us about whom we should look to for help and relief?[3]

Joseph Smith taught that we can understand all parables in this way "if we will but *open our eyes,* and read with candor."[4] In particular, we can watch for ways in which the temple symbols testify of the Savior and his atonement. I find it interesting that the word *Jesus* is spoken only a few times during the presentation of the endowment, and yet, if we watch for them, we will see references to him nearly everywhere, in some very solemn and personal ways. The temple is all about the Savior and what he has done for us.

KEY 10: A VALID INTERPRETATION OF A SYMBOL IS COMPATIBLE WITH THE SCRIPTURES AND GOSPEL TEACHINGS

The proper interpretation of temple symbols will always agree with the principles of the gospel as outlined in the scriptures and the words of the prophets. If we come to some other understanding, we can rest assured that we have it wrong, so we need to exercise caution. As the apostle Peter wrote, "No prophecy of the scripture is of any *private interpretation*. For the prophecy came not in old time by the will of man: but holy men of God spake as they were moved by the Holy Ghost" (2 Peter 1:20–21). In other words, we need to understand the endowment on its own terms and not force our own interpretations upon it. The endowment was *designed* to teach us *certain things;* we should try to understand those things and not fall into the condition of those who "despised the words of plainness, . . . and sought for things that they could not understand. Wherefore, because of their blindness, which blindness came by *looking beyond the mark,* they must needs fall; for God hath taken away his plainness from them, and delivered unto them many things which they

---

3. For more about the underlying meaning of this parable, see John W. Welch, "The Good Samaritan: Forgotten Symbols," *Ensign,* February 2007.

4. http://josephsmithpapers.org, Letter to the Elders of the Church, December 1835, 226.

cannot understand, because they desired it. And because they desired it God hath done it, that they may stumble" (Jacob 4:14).

Elder Gerald N. Lund warned that we must "fit the interpretation of any symbol into the overall scheme of gospel knowledge. No matter how clever, or how logical, or how ingenious our interpretation of a particular symbol may be, if it contradicts what is revealed in other places, we can assume it is wrong" ("Understanding Scriptural Symbols," 24).

TEMPLE THEMES

We can better understand the meaning of temple symbols if we consider them in the context of temple themes. The endowment tells a story, and the theme of any story is its underlying message or main idea. Often, a story has more than one theme. For example, the main theme of Shakespeare's play *Romeo and Juliet* is the power of love, with accompanying themes of sacrifice, contention, and so on.

The overriding theme of the temple is humanity's fall from paradise, our sojourn in the lone and dreary world, and our rescue from that world through the Savior's atonement. Moroni summarized: "Behold, [God] created Adam, and by Adam came the fall of man. And because of the fall of man came Jesus Christ, even the Father and the Son; and because of Jesus Christ came the redemption of man. And because of the redemption of man, which came by Jesus Christ, they are brought back into the presence of the Lord" (Mormon 9:12–13).

The story of Adam and Eve is our *individual* story as well. Each of us walked and talked with God in the premortal life. After our mortal birth, we lived in the innocence of childhood. Then, as adults, we left our home to earn our bread by the sweat of our brow (see Moses 5:1). Now, in our difficulties, we may turn to God, seek his messengers, and ultimately find the gospel. (Even those born in the Church must go through this process, for conversion is an individual matter.) We may marry and have children. We will certainly be confronted by Satan and learn by experience to know good from evil. As we mature in understanding and virtue, we may be sanctified by the Spirit, eventually becoming the kind of people who can dwell in celestial glory. Ultimately, we will die and, in the spirit world, await the resurrection. Pondering the endowment from this individual point of view can bring important insights, helping us become better people *in this life*.

Other temple themes include order and creation, apostasy and restoration, truth versus falsehood, God's love for his children, and the centrality and overriding importance of the Atonement. We can better understand the temple symbols as we ponder their relation to the various themes represented in the endowment. We can make this a conscious exercise, focusing on a particular theme and then considering a particular symbol in relation to that theme. As we do that, our understanding will grow.

Elder Russell M. Nelson taught,

Each temple is a house of learning.
THERE WE ARE **TAUGHT** IN THE MASTER'S WAY.
His way differs from modes of others. His way is ancient and
rich with symbolism. We can learn much by pondering the reality
for which each symbol stands.

The teachings of the temple are
beautifully simple and simply beautiful.

They are understood by the humble,
yet they can excite the intellect of the brightest minds."

("PERSONAL PREPARATION FOR TEMPLE BLESSINGS," 33)

With that in mind, let us proceed to examine some of these central themes and symbols.

The Departure of Abraham, *by Jozsef Molnar. Oil on canvas, 1850.*

"I SOUGHT FOR THE BLESSINGS"

An 1850 painting by Jozsef Molnar depicts Abraham's departure from Haran as described in the book of Genesis:

> Now the Lord had said unto Abram, Get thee out of thy country, and from thy kindred, and from thy father's house, unto a land that I will shew thee: and I will make of thee a great nation, . . . and in thee shall all families of the earth be blessed. So Abram departed, as the Lord had spoken unto him; . . . and Abram was seventy and five years old when he departed out of Haran. [Genesis 12:1–4]

The book of Abraham in the Pearl of Great Price gives more detail about Abraham's reasons for leaving:

> In the land of the Chaldeans, at the residence of my fathers, I, Abraham, saw that it was needful for me to obtain another place of residence; and, finding there was greater happiness and peace and rest for me, I sought for the blessings of the fathers, and the right whereunto I should be ordained to administer the same; having been myself a follower of righteousness, desiring also to be one who possessed great knowledge, and to be a greater follower of righteousness, and to possess a greater knowledge, and to be a father of many nations, a prince of peace. [Abraham 1:1–2]

After much seeking, Abraham found the blessings he so greatly desired:

> I, Abraham, . . . prayed unto the Lord, and the Lord appeared unto me, and said unto me: Arise, . . . for I have purposed to take thee away out of Haran, and to make of thee a minister to bear my name in a strange land which I will give unto thy seed after thee for an everlasting possession, when they hearken to my voice. . . .

And I will make of thee a great nation, and I will bless thee above measure, and make thy name great among all nations, and thou shalt be a blessing unto thy seed after thee, that in their hands they shall bear this ministry and Priesthood unto all nations;

And I will bless them through thy name; for as many as receive this Gospel shall be called after thy name, and shall be accounted thy seed, and shall rise up and bless thee, as

Vienna Genesis, folio 8. Tempera on parchment, about 1560. God reaches out from heaven, showing Abraham that his posterity will be as numerous as the stars.

their father; . . . and *in thee* (that is, in thy Priesthood) and *in thy seed* (that is, thy Priesthood) . . . shall all the families of the earth be blessed, even with the blessings of the Gospel, which are the blessings of salvation, even of life eternal.

Now, after the Lord had withdrawn from speaking to me, and withdrawn his face from me, I said in my heart: Thy servant has sought thee earnestly; now I have found thee. [Abraham 2:6–12]

These are the blessings that we, too, seek—the blessings of Abraham, Isaac, and Jacob. They are found in the house of the Lord.

"WHO SHALL ASCEND INTO THE HILL OF THE LORD?"

The psalmist described those who may enter the Lord's house: "Who shall ascend into the hill of the Lord? or who shall stand in his holy place? He that hath clean hands, and a pure heart; who hath not lifted up his soul unto vanity, nor sworn deceitfully" (Psalm 24:3–4).

"BE YE CLEAN"

In 1831 the Lord commanded the members of his church: "Go ye out from Babylon. Be ye clean that bear the vessels of the Lord" (D&C 133:5). A year later, in Kirtland, Ohio, the command was more explicit:

> I give unto you, who are the first laborers in this last kingdom, a commandment that you assemble yourselves together, and organize yourselves, and prepare yourselves, and sanctify yourselves; yea, purify your hearts, and cleanse your hands and your feet before me, that I may make you clean; that I may testify unto your Father, and your God, and my God, that you are clean from the blood of this wicked generation. [D&C 88:74–75]

In the New Testament, following the Last Supper,

> Jesus . . . laid aside his garments; and took a towel, and girded himself.
>
> After that he poureth water into a basin, and began to wash the disciples' feet, and to wipe them with the towel wherewith he was girded.
>
> Then cometh he to Simon Peter: and Peter saith unto him, Lord, dost thou wash my feet?
>
> Jesus answered and said unto him, What I do thou knowest not now; but thou shalt know hereafter.
>
> Peter saith unto him, Thou shalt never wash my feet.

Christ Washing the Disciples' Feet, by Albrecht Dürer, Woodcut, about 1510. Here, Peter asks the Savior to wash his head as well

Jesus answered him, If I wash thee not, thou hast no part with me.

Simon Peter saith unto him, Lord, not my feet only, but also my hands and my head.

Jesus saith to him, He that is washed needeth not save to wash his feet, but is clean every whit. . . .

So after he had washed their feet, and had taken his garments, and was set down again, he said unto them, Know ye what I have done to you? [John 13:3–12]

"OIL OF GLADNESS"

In addition to ritual washing, early Christians also anointed with oil. Cyril of Jerusalem (A.D. 313–386) explained that church members were known as Christians because of the anointing they had received, for the Greek title *Christ* means "anointed one" (as does *Messiah* in Hebrew):

As Christ . . . was anointed with an ideal oil of gladness, that is, with the Holy Ghost, . . . so you were anointed with ointment, having been made partakers and fellows of Christ. . . . You were first anointed on the forehead, . . . that with unveiled face ye might reflect as a mirror the glory of the Lord. Then on your ears; that you might receive the ears which are quick to hear the Divine Mysteries. . . . Then on the nostrils; that receiving the sacred ointment ye may say, We are to God a sweet savour of Christ, in them that are saved. Afterwards on your breast; that having put on the breast-plate of righteousness, you may stand against the wiles of the devil. For as Christ after His Baptism, and the visitation of the Holy Ghost, went forth and vanquished the adversary, so like-wise ye, after Holy Baptism and the Mystical Chrism [anointing], having put on the whole armour of the Holy Ghost [see Ephesians 6:11–17], are to stand against the power of the adversary, and vanquish it, saying, I can do all things through Christ which strengthens me. Having been counted worthy of this Holy Chrism, you are called Christians, verifying the name also by your new birth. [*Catechetical Lectures*, 21:2–5]

The apostle John also spoke of anointing, showing us that it was practiced from the earliest days of Christianity: "The anointing which ye have received of him abideth in you, and ye need not that any man teach you: but as the same anointing teacheth you of all things, and is truth, and is no lie, and even as it hath taught you, ye shall abide in him" (1 John 2:27).

Anointing of David, *by Felix-Joseph Barrias. Oil on canvas, 1842.* "Then Samuel took the horn of oil, and anointed him [to someday become king] in the midst of his brethren: and the Spirit of the Lord came upon David from that day forward" (1 Samuel 16:13).

"WHITE RAIMENT"

The Lord commanded John to write to the church at Laodicea:

> Because thou sayest, I am rich, and increased with goods, and have need of nothing; and knowest not that thou art wretched, and miserable, and poor, and blind, and naked: I counsel thee to buy of me gold tried in the fire, that thou mayest be rich; and white raiment, that thou mayest be clothed, and that the shame of thy nakedness do not appear; and anoint thine eyes with eyesalve, that thou mayest see. [Revelation 3:17–18]

Cyril of Jerusalem described the meaning of white raiment in early Christianity:

> Before you came to Baptism, your works were vanity. . . . But now, having put off your old garments, and put on those which are spiritually white, you must be continually robed in white: of course we mean not this, that you are always to wear white raiment; but you must be clad in the *garments* that are truly white and shining and spiritual, that you may say with the blessed Esaias, My soul shall be joyful in my God; for He has clothed me with a garment of salvation, and put a robe of gladness around me [Isaiah 61:10]. [*Catechetical Lectures*, 22:8]

Angels wait to clothe the Savior in white raiment after his baptism. Russian icon from the 1700s.

The Lord commanded a similar practice in Old Testament times, one still followed by orthodox Jews today:

> Speak unto the children of Israel, and bid them that they make them fringes in the borders of their garments throughout their generations, and that they put upon the fringe of the borders a ribband of blue: . . . *that ye may look upon it, and remember all the commandments of the Lord, and do them;* and that ye seek not after your own heart and your own eyes. . . . That ye may remember, and do all my commandments, and be holy unto your God. [Numbers 15:38–41]

"A NEW NAME"

In the book of Revelation, the Lord told John:

> Him that overcometh will I make a pillar in the temple of my God, and he shall go no more out: and I will write upon him the name of my God, and the name of the city of my God, which is new Jerusalem, which cometh down out of heaven from my God: and I will write upon him my new name. [Revelation 3:12]
>
> He that hath an ear, let him hear what the Spirit saith unto the churches; to him that overcometh will I give to eat of the hidden manna, and will give him a white stone, and in the stone a new name written, which no man knoweth saving he that receiveth it. [Revelation 2:17]

Joseph Smith explained: "A white stone is given to each of those who come into the celestial kingdom, whereon is a new name written, which no man knoweth save he that receiveth it. The new name is the key word" (D&C 130:11).

At this point, those with "clean hands, and a pure heart" are prepared to "ascend into the hill of the Lord" (Psalm 24:3–4).

THE HOLY ENDOWMENT

Prominently displayed on a wall of the Idaho Falls Temple is a verse from the Old Testament: "The Lord is in his holy temple: let all the earth keep silence before him" (Habakkuk 2:20). This verse reminds us of the quiet reverence we should maintain in the house of the Lord—not just for the sake of others but also for our own benefit: "I will fill this house with glory. . . . [I]n this place will I give peace" (Haggai 2:7–9).

In addition, we should remember that this sacred place does not belong to us; we are there at the Lord's invitation: "Hold thy peace at the presence of the Lord God: for the day of the Lord is at hand: for the Lord hath prepared a sacrifice, he hath bid his guests" (Zephaniah 1:7).

The Lord explained to Joseph Smith the activities and purposes for which temples are prepared:

> Verily I say unto you, that your anointings, and your washings, and your baptisms for the dead, and your solemn assemblies, and your memorials for your sacrifices by the sons of Levi, and for your oracles in your most holy places wherein you receive conversations, and your statutes and judgments, for the beginning of the revelations and foundation of Zion, and for the glory, honor, and endowment of all her municipals, are ordained by the ordinance of my holy house, which my people are always commanded to build unto my holy name. [D&C 124:39]

As the Lord's guests, we should pay close attention to the things we see and hear in the temple, for we go there to be instructed and not to instruct: "My friends and my brethren, my kindred and my people, I would . . . call your attention, that ye may hear and understand" (Mosiah 4:4). As we do so, we may learn the things the Lord wants to teach us, that we may someday be what he has brought us there to become: "If ye will obey my voice indeed, and keep my covenant,

Adoration of the Lamb, *Douce Apocalypse, folio 20*. Tempera on parchment, about 1265–1270. "A great multitude, which no man could number, of all nations, and kindreds, and people, and tongues, stood before the throne, and before the Lamb, clothed with white robes, and palms in their hands; and cried with a loud voice, saying, Salvation to our God which sitteth upon the throne, and unto the Lamb" (Revelation 7:9–10).

then ye shall be a peculiar treasure unto me above all people: for all the earth is mine: and ye shall be unto me a kingdom of priests, and an holy nation" (Exodus 19:5–6).

Joseph Smith explained:

> Here, then, is eternal life—to know the only wise and true God; and you have got to learn how to be gods yourselves, and to be kings and priests to God, the same as all gods have done before you, namely, by going from one small degree to another, and from a small capacity to a great one; from grace to grace, from exaltation to exaltation, until you attain to the resurrection of the dead, and are able to dwell in everlasting burnings, and to sit in glory, as do those who sit enthroned in everlasting power. And I want you to know that God, in the last days, while certain individuals are proclaiming His name, is not trifling with you or me. ["The King Follett Sermon"]

The Creation, by William Blake. Hand-colored relief etching, 1794. "When he prepared the heavens, I was there: when he set a compass upon the face of the depth" (Proverbs 8:27).

THE CREATION OF THE EARTH

A hand-colored etching by William Blake shows the Creator using a compass to circumscribe order out of chaos. John Milton described this process in his epic poem *Paradise Lost:*

> He took the **GOLDEN COMPASSES**, prepared
>
> In God's Eternal store, to circumscribe
>
> This Universe, and all created things:
>
> One foot he centered, and the other turned
>
> Round through the vast profundity obscure,
>
> And said, thus far extend, thus far thy bounds,
>
> *This be thy just Circumference, O World.*
>
> (7.225-29)

This description of the Creation is far different from the concept of traditional Christianity, which teaches that God created the world out of nothing. Joseph Smith commented on this impossible idea:

> You ask the learned doctors why they say the world was made out of nothing, and they will answer, "Doesn't the Bible say he created the world?" And they infer, from the word *create*, that it must have been made out of nothing. Now, the word *create* came from the word *baurau*, which

does not mean to create out of nothing; it means to organize; the same as a man would organize materials and build a ship. Hence we infer that God had materials to organize the world out of chaos—chaotic matter, which is element, and in which dwells all the glory. Element had an existence from the time He had. The pure principles of element are principles which can never be destroyed; they may be organized and re-organized, but not destroyed. They had no beginning and can have no end. ["The King Follett Sermon"]

ORDER

The Hebrew word translated as "create" actually means to differentiate, to separate, to set bounds (as with a compass, which is also called a "divider") (see Walton, *Ancient Near Eastern Thought and the Old Testament,* 183). We see this concept in the scriptural accounts of the Creation:

> God divided the light from the darkness. . . .
> And God made the firmament, and divided the waters which were under the firmament from the waters which were above the firmament. . . .
> And God said, Let the waters under the heaven be gathered together unto one place, and let the dry land appear: and it was so. [Genesis 1:4–9]

Separating one kind of thing from another creates order, and that is true whether we are organizing the kitchen junk drawer or doing the laundry. As the old saying goes, "A place for everything, and everything in its place." We might also say, "A time for everything, and everything in its time," for this is what we see in each stage of the Creation:

> I, God, said: Let there be light; and there was light . . . and the evening and the morning were the first day.
> And again, I, God, said: Let there be a firmament in the midst of the water, and it was so . . . and the evening and the morning were the second day. . . .
> And I, God, said: Let the earth bring forth grass, the herb yielding seed, the fruit tree yielding fruit, after his kind, and the tree yielding fruit, whose seed should be in itself upon the earth, and it was so. . . .
> And the evening and the morning were the third day. [Moses 2:3–13]

And so it is with each part of the process: "To every thing there is a season, and a time to every purpose under the heaven" (Ecclesiastes 3:1).

Clearly, God first *plans* and then *does,* until each task is properly finished. We see this principle in Abraham's account: "And then the Lord said: Let us go down. And they went down at the beginning, and they, that is the Gods, *organized* and *formed* the heavens and the earth" (Abraham 4:1). The accounts of the Creation provide valuable lessons about how to organize our work and our lives.

As we ponder these accounts, we should not be overly concerned about *how* the Creation was accomplished, for "in that day when the Lord shall come, he shall reveal all things—things which have passed, and hidden things which no man knew, *things of the earth, by which it was made, and the purpose and the end thereof*" (D&C 101:32–33).

God Reaches Out from Heaven to Divide and Bless the Waters. *Hand-colored woodcut in the Nuremberg Chronicle, 1493.*

PARTICIPATION

In the traditional Christian view of the Creation, God acts alone, with no participation from others. But Latter-day Saints have a different understanding:

> Now the Lord had shown unto me, Abraham, the intelligences that were organized before the world was; and among all these there were many of the noble and great ones; and God saw these souls that they were good, and he stood in the midst of them, and he said: These I will make my rulers; for he stood among those that were spirits, and he saw that they were good; and he said unto me: Abraham, thou art one of them; thou wast chosen before thou wast born.
>
> And there stood one among them that was like unto God, and he said unto those who were with him: We will go down, for there is space there, and we will take of these materials, and we will make an earth whereon these may dwell; and we will prove them herewith, to see if they will do all things whatsoever the Lord their God shall command them. [Abraham 3:22–25]

During Job's suffering, God questioned him: "Where wast thou when I laid the foundations of the earth? declare, if thou hast understanding. Who hath laid the measures thereof, if thou knowest? or who hath stretched the line upon it? Whereupon are the foundations thereof fastened? or who laid the corner stone thereof?" (Job 38:4–6). Having forgotten all, Job had no answer (as God's questions were intended to show). But God had an answer: Like all of God's children (including us), *Job was there,* participating, for "the morning stars sang together, and all the sons of God shouted for joy" (Job 38:7).

When the Morning Stars Sang Together, *by William Blake. Pen and black ink, gray wash, and watercolor over traces of graphite, about 1804–1807. Job and his companions are shown at the bottom; above them is God with the sun, moon, and morning stars.*

THE CREATION OF LIVING THINGS

Someone once asked the biologist J. B. S. Haldane what his study of nature had told him about God. He answered, "I think the Creator must have an inordinate fondness for beetles." There are probably several million different species of beetle; only about 350,000 have actually been identified. Making up about 20 percent of all animal life, many *trillions* of individual beetles live on planet earth! Our understanding of the extent of God's creations is extremely limited.

QUANTITY

The Creator's works are never-ending: "I, Abraham, talked with the Lord, face to face, as one man talketh with another; and he told me of the works which his hands had made; and he said unto me: My son, my son (and his hand was stretched out), behold I will show you all these. And he put his hand upon mine eyes, and I saw those things which his hands had made, which were many; and they multiplied before mine eyes, and I could not see the end thereof" (Abraham 3:11–12).

Does this passage not have an application in our own lives? When should we expect to rest from our own labors? Elder Parley P. Pratt expressed his feelings on the matter:

> I came home here from a foreign mission. I presented myself to our President [Brigham Young], and inquired what I should do next. "Rest," said he. If I had been set to turn the world over, to dig down a mountain, to go to the ends of the earth, or traverse the deserts of Arabia, it would have been easier than to have undertaken to rest, while the Priesthood was upon me. I have received the holy anointing, and I can never rest till the last enemy is conquered, death destroyed, and truth reigns triumphant. [In *Journal of Discourses,* 1:15]

VARIETY

Another lesson from the Creation is that the Lord likes variety. After all, there are approximately 8.7 million different species of life on earth, each with its own characteristics. Some of the differences in these characteristics are pointed out in two famous poems by William Blake, "The Lamb" and "The Tyger":

> *Little Lamb, who made thee?*
> *Dost thou know who made thee?*
> *Gave thee life and bid thee feed*
> *By the stream and o'er the mead;*
> *Gave thee clothing of delight,*
> *Softest clothing wooly bright;*
> *Gave thee such a tender voice,*
> *Making all the vales rejoice!*
> *Little Lamb, who made thee?*
> *Dost thou know who made thee? . . .*

> *Tyger, Tyger, burning bright,*
> *In the forests of the night:*
> *What immortal hand or eye*
> *Could frame thy fearful symmetry?*
> *. . . . .*
> *When the stars threw down their spears*
> *And watered heaven with their tears,*
> *Did he smile his work to see?*
> *Did he who made the Lamb make thee?*

We can understand why God created the lamb, but we may wonder why he created something as dangerous and terrible as the tiger—which, if it had the chance, would *eat* the lamb. But as President John Taylor said, "God's ways are not as the ways of man, neither are His thoughts limited by our limited thoughts or conceptions. But He does as He pleases" (in *Journal of Discourses,* 22:33). And as the psalmist sang, "O Lord, how manifold are thy works! in wisdom hast thou made them all: the earth is full of thy riches" (Psalm 104:10–24).

BEAUTY

God's creations are indeed glorious and beautiful!

And I, God, said: Let the waters bring forth abundantly the moving creature that hath life, and fowl which may fly above the earth in the open firmament of heaven. And I, God, created great whales, and every living creature that moveth, which the waters brought forth abundantly, after their kind, and every winged fowl after his kind; and I, God, saw that all things which I had created were good. . . .

And I, God, said: Let the earth bring forth the living creature after his kind, cattle, and creeping things, and beasts of the earth after their kind, and it was so; and I, God, made the beasts of the earth after their kind, and cattle after their kind, and everything which creepeth upon the earth after his kind; and I, God, saw that all these things were good. [Moses 2:20–25]

WISDOM

King Benjamin exhorted his people to "believe in God; believe that he is, and that he created all things, both in heaven and in earth; believe that he has all wisdom, and all power, both in heaven and in earth; believe that man doth not comprehend all the things which the Lord can comprehend" (Mosiah 4:9). The Prophet Joseph Smith wrote in his 1832 history:

I looked upon the sun, the glorious luminary of the earth, and also the moon, rolling in their majesty through the heavens, and also the stars shining in their courses; and the earth also upon which I stood, and the beast of the field and the fowls of heaven, and the fish of the waters; and also man walking forth upon the face of the earth in majesty and in the strength of beauty, [with] power and intelligence in governing the things which are so exceedingly great and marvelous, even in the likeness of him who created them.

And when I considered upon these things my heart exclaimed, Well hath the wise man said, it is a fool that saith in his heart there is no God [Psalm 53:1]. My heart exclaimed, All, all these bear testimony and bespeak an omnipotent and omnipresent power, a Being who maketh laws and decreeth and bindeth all things in their bounds.[1]

---

1. http://josephsmithpapers.org, Letterbook 1, 2–3.

The Creation, *Bible Historiale*, volume 1, folio 3. Tempera on parchment, 1411.

THE CREATION
OF ADAM AND EVE

On the west façade of the Cathedral of San Geminiano in Modena, Italy, is a bas-relief carving of the creation of Adam and Eve. On one of the carving's central panels, God creates Adam from "the dust of the ground"; on the other, he creates Eve from "one of [Adam's] ribs" (Genesis 2:7, 21). The carving was done in about the year 1100 by an artist known as Master Wiligelmo, and in some ways it might be considered quite primitive—almost childish, in fact—in its execution. Perhaps that is appropriate, for President Brigham Young actually saw the biblical account of this event as rather childish:

Here let me state to all philosophers of every class upon the earth, when you tell me that father Adam was made as we make adobes [mud bricks] from the earth, you tell me what I deem an idle tale. When you tell me that the beasts of the field were produced in that manner, you are speaking idle words devoid of meaning. There is no such thing in all the eternities where the Gods dwell. [In *Journal of Discourses*, 7:285–86]

But if Adam was not formed "as we make adobes," and Eve was not formed from Adam's rib, how were our first parents created? President Young explained that the story is simply figurative—that the process God used was actually quite different from that described in the Bible:

[Adam] is the first of the human family; and when he took a tabernacle, it was begotten by his Father in heaven, after the same manner as the tabernacles of Cain, Abel, and the rest of the sons and daughters of Adam and Eve. [In *Journal of Discourses*, 1:50–51]

Bas-relief marble carving, Cathedral of San Geminiano, Modena, Italy. On the left, God comes into the world he has just created, proclaiming (in Latin), "I am the light of the world, the true way, everlasting life." In the next panel, he creates Adam from "the dust of the ground"; then he creates Eve from "one of [Adam's] ribs" (Genesis 2:7, 21). On the right, Adam and Eve partake of the forbidden fruit, hiding their nakedness with fig leaves.

Certain verses of scripture also support this idea. For example, the book of Moses notes, "This is the genealogy of the sons of Adam, who was the son of God, with whom God, himself, conversed" (Moses 6:22; see Luke 3:38).

The Prophet Joseph Smith taught, "Where was there ever a son without a father? And where was there ever a father without first being a son? Wherever did a tree or anything spring into existence without a progenitor? And everything comes in this way" (*History of the Church,* 6:476).

Thus, "in the day that God created man, in the likeness of God made he him; in the image of his own body, male and female, created he them, . . . in the day when they were created and became living souls in the land" (Moses 6:8–9). And of course, "in the image of his own body, male and female, created he them" implies that God did not create on his own. As Eliza R. Snow wrote in her poem "Invocation, or the Eternal Father and Mother" (which we know as "O My Father"):

In the heav'ns are parents single?

NO, THE THOUGHT MAKES REASON STARE;

Truth is reason—truth eternal

Tells me I've a *Mother* there.

(*POEMS, RELIGIOUS, HISTORICAL, AND POLITICAL,* 1:1-2; SEE *HYMNS,* 292)

Elder Milton R. Hunter claimed that the "stupendous truth of the existence of a Heavenly Mother" and the "complete realization that we are the offspring of Heavenly Parents" provided "a more complete understanding of man especially regarding his person and relationship to Deity . . . than could be found in all of the holy scriptures combined" (*The Gospel through the Ages,* 98–99). Elder Parley P. Pratt summarized:

When Paradise was lost by sin; when man was driven from the face of his heavenly Father, to toil, and droop, and die; when heaven was veiled from view; and, with few exceptions, man was no longer counted worthy to retain the knowledge of his heavenly origin; then, darkness veiled the past and future from the heathen mind; man neither knew himself, from whence he came, nor whither he was bound. At length a Moses came, who knew his God, and would fain have led

Adam and Eve in the Garden of Eden, *by Wenzel Peter. Oil on canvas, about 1800.*

mankind to know Him too, and see Him face to face. But they could not receive His heavenly laws, or bide His presence. Thus the holy man was forced again to veil the past in mystery, and in the beginning of his history, assign to man an earthly origin.

Man, moulded from the earth, as a brick!

Woman, manufactured from a rib!

Thus, parents still would fain conceal from budding manhood the mysteries of procreation, or the sources of life's ever-flowing river, by relating some childish tale of new born life, engendered in the hollow trunk of some old tree, or springing with spontaneous growth like mushrooms from out the heaps of rubbish. O man! When wilt thou cease to be a child in knowledge? [*Key to the Science of Theology,* 50]

Top of the Tree of Jesse. *Stained-glass window, Chartres Cathedral.*

THE TREE OF LIFE

The Garden of Eden must have been a glorious place, filled with all manner of fruits, flowers, and vegetation. These did not spring up from nothing but were cultivated by the Lord:

I, the Lord God, *planted a garden* eastward in Eden, and there I put the man whom I had formed. And out of the ground made I, the Lord God, to grow every tree, *naturally*, that is pleasant to the sight of man; . . . and man saw that it was good for food. And I, the Lord God, planted the tree of life also in the midst of the garden, and also the tree of knowledge of good and evil. [Moses 3:8–9]

Elder Parley P. Pratt wrote:

A Royal Planter now descends from yonder world of older date, and bearing in his hand the choice seeds of the older Paradise, he plants them in the virgin soil of our new-born earth. They grow and flourish there, and, bearing seed, replant themselves, and thus clothe the naked earth with scenes of beauty and the air with fragrant incense. [*Key to the Science of Theology,* 51]

Adam and Eve were forbidden to eat the fruit of the tree of knowledge, but in their immortal state they *were* permitted to eat of the tree of life. But what is that tree?

Isaiah prophesied:

There shall come forth a rod out of the stem of Jesse, and a Branch shall grow out of his roots: and the spirit of the Lord shall rest upon him, the spirit of wisdom and understanding, the spirit of counsel and might, the spirit of knowledge and of the fear of the Lord. [Isaiah 11:1–2]

Tree of Jesse. *Stained-glass window, Chartres Cathedral.*

Jesse, of course, was the father of King David, so the prophecy refers to the royal genealogical line into which the Savior was eventually born. A window at Chartres Cathedral depicts this family tree, with Jesse sleeping while the tree grows from his loins.

The final "fruit" of this tree is the Savior, who is shown at the top of the tree with his mother, Mary, just below him (see 1 Nephi 11:13–22). Thus, the ultimate meaning of this tree is Jesse's posterity, particularly in the person of the Savior—which may more fully explain God's first commandment to Adam and Eve: "Be fruitful, and multiply, and replenish the earth" (Moses 2:28). They had to obey that commandment so the Savior could be born. Doing so, of course, also meant that *we* could be born: "After Adam and Eve had partaken of the forbidden fruit they were driven out of the garden of Eden, to till the earth. And they have brought forth children; yea, even the family of all the earth" (2 Nephi 2:19–20).

THE TREE OF KNOWLEDGE

A magnificent painting by New York artist Thomas Cole shows Adam and Eve as tiny figures expelled from paradise and cast into the lone and dreary world. What could have caused such a seeming tragedy? To understand, we start at the beginning, in the premortal world:

> Because that Satan rebelled against me, and sought to destroy the agency of man, which I, the Lord God, had given him, and also, that I should give unto him mine own power; . . . I caused that he should be cast down; and he became Satan, yea, even the devil, the father of all lies, to deceive and to blind men, and to lead them captive at his will, even as many as would not hearken unto my voice. [Moses 4:3–4]

So it was that Adam and Eve were introduced into a world where Satan had already taken hold, even in the midst of paradise. No doubt he considered it his own kingdom, his own possession, although it did not belong to him: "The earth is the Lord's, and the fulness thereof" (Psalm 24:1). The Lord told Joseph Smith, "The devil was before Adam, for he rebelled against me, saying, Give me thine honor, which is my power; and also a third part of the hosts of heaven turned he away from me because of their agency" (D&C 29:36).

Fall of the Rebel Angels, by Sebastian Ricci. Oil on canvas, about 1720. The angel with the sword is Michael (see Revelation 12:7).

FORBIDDEN FRUIT

Knowing of Satan's presence in paradise, God gave our first parents an additional commandment: "Of every tree of the garden thou mayest freely eat, but of the tree of the knowledge of good and evil, thou shalt not eat of it, nevertheless, thou mayest choose for thyself, for it is given unto thee; but, remember that I forbid it, for in the day thou eatest thereof thou shalt surely die" (Moses 3:16–17).

The prophet Lehi provides important commentary on the reason for this prohibition:

> To bring about [God's] eternal purposes in the end of man, after he had created our first parents, and the beasts of the field and the fowls of the air, and in fine, all things which are created, it must needs be that there was an opposition; even the forbidden fruit in opposition to the tree of life; the one being sweet and the other bitter. Wherefore, the Lord God gave unto man that he should act for himself. Wherefore, man could not act for himself save it should be that he was enticed by the one or the other. [2 Nephi 2:15–16]

And who would do the enticing?

> I, Lehi, according to the things which I have read, must needs suppose that an angel of God, according to that which is written, had fallen from heaven; wherefore, he became a devil, having sought that which was evil before God. And because he had fallen from heaven, and had become miserable forever, he sought also the misery of all mankind. [2 Nephi 2:17–18]

The book of Moses continues the fascinating story:

> Now the serpent was more subtle than any beast of the field which I, the Lord God, had made. And Satan put it into the heart of the serpent, (for he had drawn away many after him,) and he sought also to beguile Eve, for he knew not the mind of God, wherefore he sought to destroy the world.
>
> And he said unto the woman: Yea, hath God said—Ye shall not eat of every tree of the garden? (And he spake by the mouth of the serpent.)
>
> And the woman said unto the serpent: We may eat of the fruit of the trees of the garden; but of the fruit of the tree which thou beholdest in the midst of the garden, God hath said—Ye shall not eat of it, neither shall ye touch it, lest ye die.
>
> And the serpent said unto the woman: Ye shall not surely die; for God doth know that in the day ye eat thereof, then your eyes shall be opened, and ye shall be as gods, knowing good and evil. [Moses 4:5–11]

Adam and Eve are exceedingly modest in this painting, detail, by Jan Brueghel the Younger. Oil on canvas, about 1640.

It was true that their eyes would be opened to know good and evil—how true they had no idea! But it was not true that they would "not surely die." Alma explains why this was so:

> If it had been possible for Adam to have partaken of the fruit of the tree of life at that time, there would have been no death, and the word would have been void, making God a liar, for he said: If thou eat thou shalt surely die.
>
> And we see that death comes upon mankind, . . . which is the temporal death; nevertheless there was a space granted unto man in which he might repent; therefore this life became a probationary state; a time to prepare to meet God; a time to prepare for that endless state . . . which is after the resurrection of the dead. . . .
>
> And now behold, if it were possible that our first parents could have gone forth and partaken of the tree of life they would have been forever miserable, having no preparatory state; and thus the plan of redemption would have been frustrated, and the word of God would have been void, taking none effect.
>
> But behold, it was not so; but it was appointed unto men that they must die; and after death, they must come to judgment, even that same judgment of which we have spoken, which is the end. [Alma 12:23–27]

The story continues:

> And when the woman saw that the tree was good for food, and that it became pleasant to the eyes, and a tree to be desired to make her wise, she took of the fruit thereof, and did eat, and also gave unto her husband with her, and he did eat. And the eyes of them both were opened, and they knew that they had been naked. And they sewed fig-leaves together and made themselves aprons. [Moses 4:12–13]

Why fig leaves? A Jewish tradition identifies the tree of knowledge as a fig tree and the fig as a symbol of fertility.[1] That may be why, when the Savior encountered an unfruitful fig tree, he cursed it (see Mark 11:12–20).

---

1. Genesis Rabbah 19:6c; Berachos 40a; Sanhedrin 70a; Lightbown, *Carlo Crivelli*, 21. The idea that the forbidden fruit was an apple may have originated later as a Latin pun: by eating the *malum* (apple), Adam and Eve brought *mālum* (evil) into the world.

On the frescoed ceiling of the Sistine Chapel, Michelangelo depicted the tree of knowledge as a fig tree.

The record of Adam and Eve goes on:

And they heard the voice of the Lord God, as they were walking in the garden, in the cool of the day; and Adam and his wife went to hide themselves from the presence of the Lord God amongst the trees of the garden.

And I, the Lord God, called unto Adam, and said unto him: Where goest thou?

And he said: I heard thy voice in the garden, and I was afraid, because I beheld that I was naked, and I hid myself.

And I, the Lord God, said unto Adam: Who told thee thou wast naked? Hast thou eaten of the tree whereof I commanded thee that thou shouldst not eat, if so thou shouldst surely die?

And the man said: The woman thou gavest me, and commandest that she should remain with me, she gave me of the fruit of the tree and I did eat.

And I, the Lord God, said unto the woman: What is this thing which thou hast done? And the woman said: The serpent beguiled me, and I did eat.

And I, the Lord God, said unto the serpent: Because thou hast done this thou shalt be cursed above all cattle, and above every beast of the field; upon thy belly shalt thou go, and dust shalt thou eat all the days of thy life; and I will put enmity between thee and the woman, between thy seed and her seed; and he shall bruise thy head, and thou shalt bruise his heel. [Moses 4:14–21]

Expulsion from the Garden of Eden, *by Thomas Cole. Oil on canvas, 1828.*

DRIVEN OUT

As a result of their transgression, Adam and Eve were no longer allowed to remain in paradise:

> I, the Lord God, said unto mine Only Begotten: Behold, the man is become as one of us to know good and evil; and now lest he put forth his hand and partake also of the tree of life, and eat and live forever, therefore I, the Lord God, will send him forth from the Garden of Eden, to till the ground from whence he was taken. [Moses 4:28–29]

Lehi continues his explanation:

> Now, behold, if Adam had not transgressed he would not have fallen, but he would have remained in the garden of Eden. And all things which were created must have remained in the same state in which they were after they were created; and they must have remained forever, and had no end.
>
> And they would have had no children; wherefore they would have remained in a state of innocence, having no joy, for they knew no misery; doing no good, for they knew no sin.
>
> But behold, all things have been done in the wisdom of him who knoweth all things. Adam fell that men might be; and men are, that they might have joy. [2 Nephi 2:21–25]

In the end, all of this was done for our benefit—so that we could be born into the world:

> And in that day the Holy Ghost fell upon Adam, which beareth record of the Father and the Son, saying: I am the Only Begotten of the Father from the beginning, henceforth and forever, that as thou hast fallen thou mayest be redeemed, and all mankind, even as many as will.
>
> And in that day Adam blessed God and was filled, and began to prophesy concerning all the families of the earth, saying: Blessed be the name of God, for because of my transgression my eyes are opened, and in this life I shall have joy, and again in the flesh I shall see God.
>
> And Eve, his wife, heard all these things and was glad, saying: Were it not for our transgression we never should have had seed, and never should have known good and evil, and the joy of our redemption, and the eternal life which God giveth unto all the obedient. [Moses 5:9–11]

It was necessary for us to experience mortality, to exercise our agency and pass through sorrow that we might know the good from the evil. With that experience came physical and spiritual death. But God has provided for our rescue from what would otherwise be a hopeless situation. Lehi continues:

> And the Messiah cometh in the fulness of time, that he may redeem the children of men from the fall. And because that they are redeemed from the fall they have become free forever, knowing good from evil; to act for themselves and not to be acted upon, save it be by the punishment of the law at the great and last day, according to the commandments which God hath given.
>
> Wherefore, men are free according to the flesh; and all things are given them which are expedient unto man. And they are free to choose liberty and eternal life, through the great Mediator of all men, or to choose captivity and death, according to the captivity and power of the devil; for he seeketh that all men might be miserable like unto himself. [2 Nephi 2:26–27]

We still live in that condition today. President Joseph Fielding Smith taught:

> When Adam passed out of the Garden of Eden, then the earth became a telestial world, and it is of that order today. I do not mean a telestial glory such as will be found in telestial worlds after their resurrection, but a telestial condition which has been from the days of Adam until now and will continue until Christ comes. [*Doctrines of Salvation,* 1:85]

"COATS OF SKINS"

After the fall of Adam and Eve, God "drove out the man; and he placed at the east of the garden of Eden Cherubims, and a flaming sword which turned every way, to keep the way of the tree of life" (Genesis 3:24). But God did not leave them defenseless: "Unto Adam also and to his wife did the Lord God make coats of skins, and clothed them" (Genesis 3:21). A footnote for this verse states that the Hebrew word translated as "coats" can also mean "garments, or tunics."

Where did God get those skins? Since death had come into the world, he must have killed and skinned an animal. We know that Adam and Eve later offered sacrifice (see Moses 5:5–9), so perhaps at this point they were taught the practice by God. If so, and if that sacrifice was "a similitude of the sacrifice of the Only Begotten" (Moses 5:7), then we might see those coats of skins as representing the Savior, whose ultimate sacrifice covers our sins. As Isaiah wrote, "I will greatly rejoice in the Lord, my soul shall be joyful in my God; for he hath clothed me with the garments of salvation" (Isaiah 61:10).

The Angel of the Divine Presence Clothing Adam and Eve with Coats of Skins, *by William Blake. Watercolor over pencil, 1803.*
Note the altars of sacrifice on each side of the picture.

SATAN'S REIGN OF TERROR

We who live in relative peace and safety can hardly comprehend the extent of man's inhumanity to man in every time and nation. Satan has continually turned military, political, corporate, social, and religious power to his advantage, seeking to destroy "the agency of man, which . . . God, had given him" (Moses 4:3). Joseph Smith wrote, "We have learned by sad experience that it is the nature and disposition of almost all men, as soon as they get a little authority, as they suppose, they will immediately begin to exercise unrighteous dominion" (D&C 121:39). These are the things that make God weep:

And it came to pass that the God of heaven looked upon the residue of the people, and he wept. . . . And Enoch said unto the Lord: How is it that thou canst weep, seeing thou art holy, and from all eternity to all eternity? . . .

The Lord said unto Enoch: Behold these thy brethren; they are the workmanship of mine own hands, and I gave unto them their knowledge, in the day I created them; and in the Garden of Eden, gave I unto man his agency;

And unto thy brethren have I said, and also given commandment, that they should love one another, and that they should choose me, their Father; but behold, they are without affection, and they hate their own blood. . . . Wherefore should not the heavens weep, seeing these shall suffer? [Moses 7:28–37]

Mormon wrote, "O how foolish, and how vain, and how evil, and devilish, and how quick to do iniquity, and how slow to do good, are the children of men; yea, how quick to hearken unto the words of the evil one, and to set their hearts upon the vain things of the world!" (Helaman 12:4). Elder Neal A. Maxwell observed:

We are in a period in which so many are fascinated by charisma or seek for empowerment. Power to do what, however? This is the relevant question. Clever and evil, Hitler and Stalin (along with their combined henchmen) certainly had vast power. They helped to account for the premature losses of life in Greater Europe between 1930 and 1953 of an estimated 40–50 million people—as a result of wars and famine, massacres, purges, and exterminations. ["The Disciple-Scholar," 17]

The Course of Empire: Destruction,
by Thomas Cole. Oil on canvas, 1836.
The artist described this painting as "a
tempest,–a battle, and the burning of the
city–towers falling, arches broken, vessels
wrecking in the harbour. . . . This is the
scene of destruction or vicious state [of
civilization]" (Letter to Luman Reed, 18
September 1833, in Noble, The Life and
Works of Thomas Cole, *130).*

The Lord has warned us:

No power or influence can or ought to be maintained by virtue of the priesthood, only by persuasion, by long-suffering, by gentleness and meekness, and by love unfeigned; by kindness, and pure knowledge, which shall greatly enlarge the soul without hypocrisy, and without guile. [D&C 121:41–42]

The rights of the priesthood are inseparably connected with the powers of heaven, and . . . the powers of heaven cannot be controlled nor handled only upon the principles of righteousness. [D&C 121:36]

As we heed that warning, Satan will have "no power over the hearts of the people, for they dwell in righteousness," but "all those who belong to the kingdom of the devil are they who need fear, and tremble, and quake; they are those who must be brought low in the dust; they are those who must be consumed as stubble; and this is according to the words of the prophet" (1 Nephi 22:26, 23).

CUTTING A COVENANT

In our modern world, where people purchase steaks and roasts in neatly sealed packages at the supermarket, it is difficult for most of us to understand what it really means to kill an animal. Taking a life is a serious matter, and in ancient Israel, sacrifice followed a specific sequence:

After an animal had been selected, his throat was cut across with one single blow. [This humane, nearly painless procedure led quickly to unconsciousness and death.] The next ceremony was to [open] the breast . . . and pluck out the heart, and if there were the least imperfection, the body would be considered unclean. The animal was then divided into two parts [at the abdomen], and placed north and south, that the parties to the covenant might pass between them from east to west. [Oliver, *Historical Landmarks,* 2:179][2]

All such sacrifices, of course, ultimately had reference to the "great and last sacrifice" of the Savior (Alma 34:14), and they were associated with making covenants. The Bible Dictionary notes under "Covenant":

---

2. Details of the ritual are preserved in the Talmud, tractates Tamid and Zevahim.

Agnus Dei ("*Lamb of God*"), by Josefa de Ayala. Oil on canvas, about 1670–1684. The Latin inscription at the bottom of the painting translates as "Slain from the foundation of the world" (Revelation 13:8).

[A covenant] denotes an agreement between persons (1 Sam. 23:18) or nations (1 Sam. 11:1); more often between God and man; but in this latter case it is important to notice that the two parties to the agreement do not stand in the relation of independent and equal contractors. God in His good pleasure fixes the terms, which man accepts. . . . The gospel is so arranged that principles and ordinances are received by covenant, placing the recipient under strong obligation and responsibility to honor the commitment. Thus the severe consequences to Ananias and Sapphira, who deliberately broke their covenant and lied unto God (Acts 5:1–11).

The Hebrew word for "covenant," *berith,* refers to such consequences, as it is derived from a root which means "to cut." According to *Easton's Bible Dictionary,* "a covenant is a 'cutting,' with reference to the cutting or dividing of animals into two parts, and the contracting parties passing between them."

Abraham, in a dream, sees God accepting the sacrifice of the covenant.
Miniature from Petrus Comestor's Bible Historiale, tempera on vellum, 1372.
In Genesis 15, God actually passes between the pieces of the sacrifice to ratify
his covenant with Abraham (see verses 17–18).

We see an example in the book of Jeremiah, where the people of Jerusalem covenanted with King Zedekiah that they would free their slaves. In token of their covenant, they sacrificed a calf. Then "they cut the calf in twain [in two], and passed between the parts thereof; the princes of Judah, and the princes of Jerusalem, the eunuchs, and the priests, and all the people of the land . . . passed between the parts of the calf" (Jeremiah 34:18–19). The implication was that if the people did not keep their covenant, they expected to be killed just as the calf had been killed.[3]

Even today, we see the persistence of such customs in the childish oath "Cross my heart and hope to die."

The Book of Mormon notes a similar custom among the Nephites:

> When Moroni had proclaimed these words, behold, the people came running together with their armor girded about their loins, rending their garments in token, or as a covenant, that they would not forsake the Lord their God; or, in other words, if they should transgress the commandments of God, or fall into transgression, and be ashamed to take upon them the name of Christ, the Lord should rend them even as they had rent their garments. [Alma 46:21; see also v. 22][4]

---

3. See Jared T. Parker, "Cutting Covenants," in Ogden, Ludlow, and Muhlestein, *The Gospel of Jesus Christ in the Old Testament.*

4. See Thomas R. Valletta, "The Captain and the Covenant," in Nyman and Tate, *Alma.*

SIGNS AND TOKENS

The painting titled *Adoration of the Magi* (page 2) shows many people making symbolic gestures. Known as signs or tokens, such gestures are frequently used in the art of the Middle Ages to convey certain meanings, but they can be found in artwork and ritual all over the world. Many have been passed down from time immemorial, and we still use some of them, almost without thinking. For example, when a Primary teacher puts a finger to her lips to tell a child to be quiet, she is making the sign of silence, which was used anciently as a warning against revealing sacred things. When we put our hand over our heart to pledge our allegiance or when we raise our right hand in court, promising to "tell the truth, the whole truth, and nothing but the truth," we are making a sign that indicates our commitment.

Such signs are to be found all over the world, in nearly every time and culture. Hugh Nibley explained that they "are as old as the human race and represent a primordial revealed religion that has passed through alternate phases of apostasy and restoration which have left the world littered with the scattered fragments of the original structure, some more and some less recognizable, but all badly damaged and out of proper context. . . . Whatever the end result may be, it is perfectly clear by now that the same sort of thing has been going on for a very long time and in virtually all parts of the world" (*Message of the Joseph Smith Papyri*, xxvii).

The Bible often mentions these things. For example, after Noah and his family left the ark, the Lord made a covenant with them and established a token in remembrance of that covenant:

Sign of silence. Tempera on plaster, Coptic, eighth century.

I will establish my covenant with you; neither shall all flesh be cut off any more by the waters of a flood; neither shall there any more be a flood to destroy the earth.

And God said, This is the token of the covenant which I make between me and you and every living creature that is with you, for perpetual generations: I do set my bow in the cloud, and it shall be for a token of a covenant between me and the earth. And it shall come to pass, when I bring a cloud over the earth, that the bow shall be seen in the cloud: and I will remember my covenant, which is between me and you and every living creature of all flesh; and the waters shall no more become a flood to destroy all flesh. [Genesis 9:11–15]

Thanksgiving After Leaving the Ark, by Domenico Morelli. Oil on canvas, 1901.

When God made his covenant with Abraham, he gave him a new name (his previous name was Abram) and established circumcision as a token of the covenant, signifying that Abraham would be "a father of many nations," which promise would continue with his posterity after him (see Genesis 17:1–11).

When Moses and the children of Israel held the first Passover, before their release from Egyptian bondage, the Lord gave Moses these instructions with an accompanying promise:

> Speak ye unto all the congregation of Israel, saying, In the tenth day of this month they shall take to them every man a lamb, according to the house of their fathers, a lamb for an house. . . . Your lamb shall be without blemish, a male of the first year: . . . and the whole assembly of the congregation of Israel shall kill it in the evening.
>
> And they shall take of the blood, and strike it on the two side posts and on the upper door post of the houses, wherein they shall eat it. And they shall eat the flesh in that night, roast with fire, and unleavened bread; and with bitter herbs they shall eat it. . . .
>
> And the blood shall be to you for a token upon the houses where ye are: and when I see the blood, I will pass over you, and the plague shall not be upon you to destroy you, when I smite the land of Egypt. [Exodus 12:3–13]

The tokens of the passover were given to each family, but the Nephites experienced similar emblems individually, just as we do when taking the sacrament:

> The Lord spake unto them saying: Arise and come forth unto me, that ye may thrust your hands into my side, and also that ye may feel the prints of the nails in my hands and in my feet, that ye may know that I am the God of Israel, and the God of the whole earth, and have been slain for the sins of the world.
>
> And it came to pass that the multitude went forth, and thrust their hands into his side, and did feel the prints of the nails in his hands and in his feet; and this they did do, going forth *one by one* until they had all gone forth, and did see with their eyes and did feel with their hands, and did know of a surety and did bear record, that it was he, of whom it was written by the prophets, that should come. [3 Nephi 11:13–15]

The Incredulity of St. Thomas, *by Benjamin West. Oil on canvas, about 1770.*

After at first doubting the Lord's resurrection, the apostle Thomas had a similar experience:

> After eight days again his disciples were within, and Thomas with them: Then came Jesus, the doors being shut, and stood in the midst, and said, Peace be unto you. Then saith he to Thomas, Reach hither thy finger, and behold my hands; and reach hither thy hand, and thrust it into my side: and be not faithless, but believing. And Thomas answered and said unto him, My Lord and my God. [John 20:26–28]

Jesus went on to prove his identity in other ways as well:

> And *many other signs* truly did Jesus in the presence of his disciples, which are not written in this book: but these are written, that ye might believe that Jesus is the Christ, the Son of God; and that believing ye might have life through his name. [John 20:30–31]

Through the Holy Ghost [Jesus] had given commandments unto the apostles whom he had chosen: to whom also he shewed himself alive after his passion by *many infallible proofs*,[5] being seen of them forty days, and speaking of the things pertaining to the kingdom of God. [Acts 1:2–3]

ABOVE AND BELOW

Leonardo da Vinci, famous artist of the Renaissance, included in some of his paintings a gesture known as the sign of heaven. This consists simply of a finger pointing skyward. It can be seen in the artist's mural of the Last Supper (at the Convent of Santa Maria delle Grazie in Milan), his painting of John the Baptist (in the Louvre), and his drawing of Mary with her cousin Elisabeth (probably) and the infants Jesus and John the Baptist (in England's National Gallery).

This sign usually refers to the Savior, indicating either that he came from heaven or is returning to heaven, for he "ascended up on high, as also he descended below all things" (D&C 88:6).

The Last Supper, *detail, by Leonardo da Vinci. Tempera on gesso, pitch, and mastic, 1495–1498.*

St. John the Baptist, *by Leonardo da Vinci. Oil on walnut, about 1513–1516.*

---

5. The Greek word for "infallible proofs" is a derivative of *tekmerion*, which means "a sure sign," "a mark," "a token."

Mary and Elisabeth (traditionally identified as Anne, Mary's mother) with Jesus and John, by Leonardo da Vinci. Charcoal with black and white chalk on tinted paper mounted on canvas, about 1499–1500 or 1506–1508.

That idea is encapsulated in the description of the Savior's ascension in the book of Acts:

> While [the apostles] beheld, [Jesus] was taken up; and a cloud received him out of their sight. And while they looked steadfastly toward heaven as he went up, behold, two men stood by them in white apparel; which also said, Ye men of Galilee, why stand ye gazing up into heaven? this same Jesus, which is taken up from you into heaven, shall so come in like manner as ye have seen him go into heaven. [Acts 1:9–11]

We, too, once lived on high (our first estate) but have now descended to this vale of sorrow (our second estate), where we are tested and tried:

> And they who keep their first estate shall be added upon; and they who keep not their first estate shall not have glory in the same kingdom with those who keep their first estate; and they who keep their second estate shall have glory added upon their heads for ever and ever. [Abraham 3:26]

Religion mural by Charles Sprague Pearce at the Library of Congress, 1896.

THE HUMAN CONDITION

The Latin phrase *in extremis* means "in extremity," "in dire straits," or "in a tight spot," which is where we find ourselves after coming into this lone and dreary world. Faced with trials and troubles, disease and death, we struggle to reconnect with our heavenly home.

After the Fall, cast out from the Garden of Eden, our first parents were in just such a predicament. With no other recourse, their solution was to pray. As the scriptures tell us, "Adam and Eve, his wife, *called upon the name of the Lord,* and they heard the voice of the Lord from the way toward the Garden of Eden, speaking unto them, and they saw him not; *for they were shut out from his presence*" (Moses 5:4). This is the desperate condition we all must endure here in mortality. Incidents in the scriptures and Church history provide some notable illustrations.

JOSEPH SMITH IN LIBERTY JAIL

When Joseph Smith was imprisoned for four months in Liberty Jail, he and his companions described the place as "hell surrounded with demons." The dark, dirty dungeon had only straw couches to sleep on and food they described as "so filthy that we could not eat it until we were driven to it by hunger" (Jessee, "'Walls, Gates and Screeking Iron Doors,'" 25, 27). Finally, in despair, Joseph cried out, "O God, where art thou?" (D&C 121:1).

After much suffering, Joseph's prayer was answered: "My son, peace be unto thy soul; thine adversity and thine afflictions shall be but a small moment; and then, if thou endure it well, God shall exalt thee on high. . . . Thou art not yet as Job" (D&C 121:7–10).

JONAH

Jonah, fleeing from his duty of preaching to the people of Nineveh, boarded a ship bound for Tarshish—as far from Nineveh as he could possibly go. "But the Lord sent out a great wind into the sea, and there was a mighty tempest in the sea, so that the ship was like to be broken." The mariners did all they could to keep from sinking but finally decided, "Let us cast lots, that we may know for whose cause this evil is upon us." The lot, of course, "fell upon Jonah," who explained that he had "fled from the presence of the Lord" (Jonah 1:4, 7, 10).

"Then said they unto him, What shall we do unto thee, that the sea may be calm unto us? . . . And he said unto them, Take me up, and cast me forth into the sea; so shall the sea be calm unto you: for I know that for my sake this great tempest is upon you." The mariners did so, "and the sea ceased from her raging" (Jonah 1:11–12, 15). Then came an amazing experience:

Jonah and the Whale, *by Pieter Lastman. Oil on oak, 1621.*

Now the Lord had prepared a great fish to swallow up Jonah. And Jonah was in the belly of the fish three days and three nights. Then Jonah prayed unto the Lord his God out of the fish's belly, and said, I cried by reason of mine affliction unto the Lord, and he heard me; *out of the belly of hell* cried I, and *thou heardest my voice.* For thou hadst cast me into the deep, in the midst of the seas; and the floods compassed me about: all thy billows and thy waves passed over me. . . . When my soul fainted within me I remembered the Lord: and my prayer came in unto thee, *into thine holy temple.* . . . I will sacrifice unto thee with the voice of thanksgiving; I will pay that that I have vowed. Salvation is of the Lord. [Jonah 1:17–2:9]

JOB

Mentioned by the Lord to Joseph Smith in Liberty Jail, Job is a preeminent example of one who endured the trials of mortality, including the loss of his family and possessions, intense physical suffering, and condemnation by his supposed friends. In despair, he cried out to a God who, at first, seemed not to hear him at all, even though Job was "perfect and upright, and one that

feared God, and eschewed evil" (Job 1:1). Finally, realizing his utter dependence on God and his own inadequacy, "Job answered the Lord, and said, I know that thou canst do every thing, and that no thought can be withholden from thee. . . . Therefore have I uttered that I understood not; things too wonderful for me, which I knew not. *Hear, I beseech thee,* and *I will speak:* I will [ask] of thee, and declare thou unto me. I have heard of thee by the hearing of the ear: but now mine eye seeth thee. Wherefore I abhor myself, and repent in dust and ashes" (Job 42:1–6).

Job's Despair, by William Blake. Pen and black ink, gray wash, and watercolor over traces of graphite, 1805.

THE SAVIOR

Jesus himself was not exempt from our mortal condition of trials and troubles. As he explained to Joseph Smith, "I, God, have suffered these things for all, that they might not suffer if they would repent; but if they would not repent they must suffer even as I; which suffering caused myself, even God, the greatest of all, to tremble because of pain, and to bleed at every pore, and to suffer both body and spirit—and would that I might not drink the bitter cup, and shrink—nevertheless, glory be to the Father, and I partook and finished my preparations unto the children of men" (D&C 19:16–19).

All of this he did voluntarily and without help. With arms outstretched, nailed to the cross, he prayed in anguish, "*Eloi, Eloi, lama sabachthani,*" which is Aramaic for "My God, my God, why hast thou forsaken me?" (Mark 15:34; see Matthew 27:46; Psalm 22:1). But this time, the prayer brought no answer.

THE ATTITUDE OF PRAYER

Christ on the Cross, by Peter Paul Rubens. Black chalk, heightened with white and gray, on paper, about 1630–1631.

Walter Lowrie, an expert on early Christian art, wrote, "It is commonly said that the outstretched hands reflect the common attitude of prayer. It would be more correct to say that this is the characteristic attitude of the *Christian* in prayer. . . . The Christians adopted a very significant attitude in prayer, which early writers (among them Tertullian, *De orat.* 14) described as the attitude of Christ on the cross. . . . This was the attitude of the orant [person praying], and it is still the attitude of the priest at the altar" (*Art in the Early Church*, 64). Tertullian wrote that some "do not dare to raise their hands to the Lord. . . . In our case, not only do we raise them, we even spread them out, and, *imitating the Passion of our Lord*, we confess Christ as we pray" (*De Orationes* [*On Prayer*], 14).

"THE GOD OF
THIS WORLD"

After Jesus was baptized and had received the Holy Ghost (Luke 3:21–22), he was "led up of the Spirit into the wilderness to be with God" (Joseph Smith Translation, Matthew 4:1). Following a season of fasting and prayer, "he was afterward an hungred." Taking advantage of the Savior's weakened condition, "the tempter came to him" with words implying that *he* was the Only Begotten rather than Jesus: "If *thou* be the Son of God, command that these stones be made bread" (Matthew 4:2–3).

When Jesus refused, Satan tempted him to cast himself down from the pinnacle of the temple, implying that if Jesus would not do so, he didn't really believe that angels would "bear [him] up" because he was not the Messiah (see Matthew 4:6). Again Jesus refused. Then came a final, more blatant temptation:

> The devil, taking him up into an high mountain, shewed unto him all the kingdoms of the world in a moment of time. And the devil said unto him, All this power will I give thee, and the glory of them: for that is delivered unto me; and to whomsoever I will I give it. If thou therefore wilt worship me, all shall be thine. [Luke 4:5–7]

Elder Jeffrey R. Holland commented:

> Satan makes up for lack of subtlety here with the grandeur of his offer. Never mind that these kingdoms are not ultimately his to give. He simply asks of the great Jehovah, God of Heaven and Earth, "What is your price? Cheap bread you resist. Tawdry Messianic drama you resist. But no man can resist this world's wealth. Name your price." Satan is proceeding under his first article of faithlessness—the unequivocal belief that you can buy anything in this world for money. ["The Inconvenient Messiah," 71]

The Temptation of Christ, *by Juan de Flandes. Oil on panel, about 1500–1504. Note the figures on the mountain and on the pinnacle of the temple.*

Jesus, of course, refused this temptation, saying, "Get thee hence, Satan: for it is written, Thou shalt worship the Lord thy God, and him only shalt thou serve." Then "the devil leaveth him, and, behold, angels came and ministered unto him" (Matthew 4:10–11).

Similarly, after Moses had communed with God, "Satan came tempting him, saying: Moses, son of man, worship me" (Moses 1:12). When Moses refused and told him to depart, Satan "cried with a loud voice, and ranted upon the earth, and commanded, saying: *I am the Only Begotten, worship me*" (Moses 1:19). Then in the name of the *true* Only Begotten, Moses cast Satan out:

> And it came to pass that Moses began to fear exceedingly; and as he began to fear, he saw the bitterness of hell. Nevertheless, calling upon God, he received strength, and he commanded, saying: Depart from me, Satan, for this one God only will I worship, which is the God of glory.
>
> And now Satan began to tremble, and the earth shook; and Moses received strength, and called upon God, saying: In the name of the Only Begotten, depart hence, Satan.
>
> And it came to pass that Satan cried with a loud voice, with weeping, and wailing, and gnashing of teeth; and he departed hence, even from the presence of Moses, that he beheld him not. [Moses 1:20–22]

Then God explained to Moses the reason behind Satan's deception:

> That Satan, whom thou hast commanded in the name of mine Only Begotten, is the same which was from the beginning, and he came before me, saying—Behold, here am I, send me, *I will be thy Son,* and I will redeem all mankind, that one soul shall not be lost, and surely I will do it; wherefore give me thine honor.
>
> But, behold, my Beloved Son, which was my Beloved and Chosen from the beginning, said unto me—Father, thy will be done, and the glory be thine forever.
>
> Wherefore, because that Satan rebelled against me, and sought to destroy the agency of man, which I, the Lord God, had given him, and also, that I should give unto him mine own power; by the power of mine Only Begotten, I caused that he should be cast down;
>
> And he became Satan, yea, even the devil, the father of all lies, to deceive and to blind men, and to lead them captive at his will, even as many as would not hearken unto my voice. [Moses 4:1–4; italic capital S added]

So from the very beginning, Satan has tried to lead God's children astray by claiming a position that, in reality, belongs to the Savior:

Adam and Eve blessed the name of God, and they made all things known unto their sons and their daughters. And Satan came among them, saying: *I am also a Son of God*; and he commanded them, saying: Believe it not; and they believed it not, and they loved Satan more than God. And men began from that time forth to be carnal, sensual, and devilish. [Moses 5:12–13; italic capital S added]

As the apostle Paul wrote, "The god of this world hath blinded the minds of them which believe not, lest the light of the glorious gospel of Christ, who is the image of God, should shine unto them" (2 Corinthians 4:4; see also John 12:31; 14:30; 16:11).

The Blind Leading the Blind. *Oil painting after Pieter Bruegel, 1500s. "Let them alone: they be blind leaders of the blind. And if the blind lead the blind, both shall fall into the ditch" (Matthew 15:14).*

GOD'S MESSENGERS

A common theme in art from the Middle Ages and the Renaissance is the visit of three messengers to Abraham, as described in Genesis 18:1–19:

The Lord appeared unto [Abraham] in the plains of Mamre: and he sat in the tent door in the heat of the day; and he lift up his eyes and looked, and, lo, three men stood by him: and when he saw them, he ran to meet them from the tent door, and bowed himself toward the ground, and said, My Lord, if now I have found favour in thy sight, pass not away, I pray thee, from thy servant: let a little water, I pray you, be fetched, and wash your feet, and rest yourselves under the tree: and I will fetch a morsel of bread, and comfort ye your hearts. . . . And they said, So do, as thou hast said. . . .

And they said unto him, Where is Sarah thy wife? And he said, Behold, in the tent. And he said, I will certainly return unto thee according to the time of life; and, lo, Sarah thy wife shall have a son. . . .

And the men rose up from thence, and looked toward Sodom: and Abraham went with them to bring them on the way. And the Lord said, Shall I hide from Abraham that thing which I do; seeing that Abraham shall surely become a great and mighty nation, and all the nations of the earth shall be blessed in him? For I know him, that he will command his children and his household after him, and they shall keep the way of the Lord, to do justice and judgment; that the Lord may bring upon Abraham that which he hath spoken of him.

The identity of these three visitors has been the subject of much debate and speculation, but clearly they came to deliver a message to Abraham and Sarah: Even in their old age, they would have a son, through whom God's promise of "a great and mighty" posterity would be realized and

Abraham Entertaining the Three Angels, *by Rembrandt van Rijn. Etching, 1656. Abraham is on the right and the three angels on the left, with the imposing angel in the middle representing the Lord.*

all the nations of the earth would be blessed. The ultimate fulfillment of this promise is the Savior himself.

From the beginning, God has communicated with his children in this way, sending messengers with the glad news of salvation: "I, the Lord God, gave unto Adam and unto his seed, that they should not die as to the temporal death, until I . . . should send forth angels to declare unto them repentance and redemption, through faith on the name of mine Only Begotten Son" (D&C 29:42; see Moses 5:58).

Elder Jeffrey R. Holland taught:

God knew the challenges [Adam and Eve] would face [when they stepped into mortality], and He certainly knew how lonely and troubled they would sometimes feel. So He watched over His mortal family constantly, heard their prayers always, and sent prophets (and later apostles) to teach, counsel, and guide them. But in times of special need, He sent angels, divine messengers, to bless His children, reassure them that heaven was always very close and that His help was always very near. Indeed, shortly after Adam and Eve found themselves in the lone and dreary world, an angel appeared unto them, who taught them the meaning of their sacrifice and the atoning role of the promised Redeemer who was to come. ["The Ministry of Angels," 29]

According to the *Anchor Yale Bible Dictionary,* the Hebrew word most commonly translated as "angel" is *malāk,* meaning simply "messenger" or "envoy." It is from the translation of this word into Greek (*aggelos*) that we get our English word *angel.* (Both *aggelos* and *malāk* can refer to either mortal or heavenly beings.) Similarly, the word *apostle* in the original Greek (*apostolos*) means "one who is sent," or "a messenger." Unfortunately, the original apostles were not recognized as such by most of those to whom they were sent. The Savior warned them:

> If the world hate you, ye know that it hated me before it hated you. If ye were of the world, the world would love his own: but because ye are not of the world, but I have chosen you out of the world, therefore the world hateth you. Remember the word that I said unto you, The servant is not greater than his lord. If they have persecuted me, they will also persecute you. . . . But all these things will they do unto you for my name's sake, because they know not him that sent me. [John 15:18–21]

Peter, James, and John, *by Pere Serra. Tempera and gold leaf on wood, circa 1385. Peter holds his great key of authority: "I will give unto thee the keys of the kingdom of heaven" (Matthew 16:19). James holds a walking stick; on his hat is a scallop shell, a symbol of pilgrimage. John holds a reed pen: "Write the things which thou hast seen, and the things which are, and the things which shall be hereafter" (Revelation 1:19).*

Of course, the most important messenger sent from God was Jesus himself, "the messenger of the covenant, whom ye delight in" (Malachi 3:1): "In this was manifested the love of God toward us, because that God sent his only begotten Son into the world, that we might live through him. Herein is love, not that we loved God, but that he loved us, and sent his Son to be the propitiation for our sins" (1 John 4:9–10).

This is the gospel, the "good tidings of great joy, which shall be to all people" (Luke 2:10). Just as with the apostles,

The Nativity at Night, *by Geertgen tot Sint Jans. Oil on oak, about 1490.*

however, very few recognized the Savior's true character during his mortal ministry. Isaiah said he would be "despised and rejected of men" (Isaiah 53:3), and the apostle John wrote, "In him was life; and the life was the light of men. And the light shineth in darkness; and the darkness comprehended it not. . . . He was in the world, and the world was made by him, and the world knew him not" (John 1:4–10).

THE APOSTASY:
TIME OF SATAN'S POWER

After the death of the apostles came the Great Apostasy, a falling away from the truth, for those who held the keys of the kingdom were gone, and in their place came false priests and impostors. The apostle Paul, before his death, prophesied:

I know this, that after my departing shall grievous wolves enter in among you, not sparing the flock. Also of your own selves shall men arise, speaking perverse things, to draw away disciples after them. Therefore watch, and remember, that by the space of three years I ceased not to warn every one night and day with tears. [Acts 20:29–31; see 1 Corinthians 1:10–13]

With the church's division and fragmentation came the great day of Satan's power, which the Prophet Enoch saw in vision: "[Enoch] beheld Satan . . . [who] had a great chain in his hand, and it veiled the whole face of the earth with darkness; and [Satan] looked up and laughed, and his angels rejoiced" (Moses 7:26).

Eventually, as Nephi prophesied, a multitude of Christian sects and denominations arose:

It shall come to pass . . . that the churches which are built up, and not unto the Lord, when the one shall say unto the other: Behold, I, I am the Lord's; and the others shall say: I, I am the Lord's; and thus shall every one say that hath built up churches, and not unto the Lord—and they shall contend one with another; and their priests shall contend one with another, and they shall teach with their learning, and deny the Holy Ghost, which giveth utterance. And they deny the power of God, the Holy One of Israel; and they say unto the people: Hearken unto us, and hear ye our precept; . . . because of false teachers, and false doctrine, their churches have become corrupted. [2 Nephi 28:3–12]

TEACHINGS OF THE APOSTASY

Elder Dallin H. Oaks observed:

> From . . . the writings of churchmen and philosophers there came a synthesis of Greek phi-
> losophy and Christian doctrine in which the orthodox Christians of that day lost the fulness of
> truth about the nature of God and the Godhead. The consequences persist in the various creeds
> of Christianity, which declare a Godhead of only one being and which describe that single being
> or God as "incomprehensible" and "without body, parts, or passions." In the process of what we call
> the Apostasy, the tangible, personal God described in the Old and New Testaments was replaced
> by the abstract, incomprehensible deity defined by compromise with the speculative principles of
> Greek philosophy. ["Apostasy and Restoration," 84]

One of the earliest of the churchmen and philosophers mentioned by Elder Oaks was Augustine
of Hippo (354–430), whose books *Confessions* and *The City of God* had an enormous impact on
Christianity. The most important, however, was Thomas Aquinas (1225–1274), a Dominican friar
and theologian who sought to reconcile the philosophies of Plato and Aristotle with the teachings
of the Catholic church, most notably in his 3,500-page masterwork, *Summa Theologica* ("Summary
of Theology"), which cites numerous Christian, Muslim, Hebrew, and pagan philosophers. At the
Council of Trent (1545–1563), his *Summa* was placed on the altar alongside the Bible, showing the
extraordinarily high esteem in which his work was held. A painting done by Carlo Crivelli in 1476
depicts Aquinas holding the church in one hand and his *Summa* in the other.[1]

Elder Erastus Snow provided an interesting summary of the ideas that resulted from the syn-
thesis of Greek philosophy with the teachings of scripture:

> [Traditional Christianity declares] that God is a spirit, without body, parts and passions. His
> centre is everywhere, his circumference is nowhere. His form may be best described in the quaint
> language of Parley P. Pratt, "A footless stocking without a leg," sitting upon the top of a topless
> throne, far beyond the bounds of time and space. . . . And we are asked to believe in, render obe-
> dience to, and worship this being. The careful thinker says, "I cannot; it is impossible for me to
> believe in a being that has neither body, parts, nor passions, and that is located nowhere; I cannot

---

1. Interestingly, after a revelatory experience just a few months before his death, Aquinas remarked, "All that I have written
[now] seems like straw to me" (Davies, *Thought of Thomas Aquinas,* 9).

Saint Thomas Aquinas,
*altarpiece painting by
Carlo Crivelli. Tempera
on poplar, 1476.*

conceive of him." . . . We do not wonder that the reflecting, careful thinker should repudiate their crude notions. [In *Journal of Discourses,* 19:268]

Joseph Smith explained, "The idea that the Father and the Son dwell in a man's heart is an old sectarian notion, and is false" (D&C 130:3).

Another false idea, most notably taught by church reformer John Calvin, is that people are saved solely through God's good pleasure, *not* through faith in the Savior and his sanctifying power:

God by his eternal and immutable counsel determined once for all those whom it was his pleasure one day to admit to salvation, and those whom, on the other hand, it was his pleasure to doom to destruction. We maintain that this counsel, as regards the elect, is founded on his free mercy, *without any respect to human worth,* while those whom he dooms to destruction are excluded from access to life by a just and blameless, but at the same time incomprehensible judgment. [*Institutes of Christian Religion,* 3:21:7]

Before the restoration of the gospel, false teachings about the devil were also common. For example, in *The Pilgrim's Progress,* published in 1678, John Bunyan describes Satan as a monster, Apollyon (which Revelation 9:11 gives as one of his names):

The monster was hideous to behold: he was clothed with scales like a fish, and they are his pride; he had wings like a dragon, feet like a bear, and out of his belly came fire and smoke, and his mouth was as the mouth of a lion.

Similarly, the "torments of hell" were described as literal realities:

Consider . . . what damnation is, and how many and how great the miseries it involves. A dying life, or rather a living death; a darksome prison, . . . and a land of horror and misery; *a lake of fire and brimstone; a bottomless pit;* . . . *a body always burning, and never consumed.* . . . This is a short description, drawn for the most part from God's unerring word, of the miseries which eternal damnation imports; this is the bitter cup of which all the sinners of the earth must drink. [Challoner, *Think Well On't,* 37]

Thankfully, Latter-day Saints do not believe in any such place. Joseph Smith taught, "A man is his own tormentor and his own condemner. Hence the saying, They shall go into the lake that burns with fire and brimstone. The torment of disappointment in the mind is as exquisite as a lake burning with fire and brimstone. I say, so is the torment of man."[2]

SELLING THE SACRED

A nineteenth-century fresco in the Altlerchenfelder Church in Vienna, Austria, shows Judas betraying the Savior with a kiss. Behind his back, Judas clutches a purse containing the thirty

The Betrayal
of Judas,
Altlerchenfelder
Church in
Vienna, Austria.
Fresco, 1800s.

---

2. http://josephsmithpapers.org, History, 1838–1856, volume E-1 [1 July 1843–30 April 1844], 1976.

pieces of silver he was paid for his treachery. The image is a powerful reminder of where our loyalties should lie. As Hugh Nibley wrote, "Wealth is a jealous master who will not be served half-heartedly and will suffer no rival—not even God: 'Ye cannot serve God and Mammon' (Matthew 6:24). In return for unquestioning obedience, wealth promises security, power, position, and honors, in fact anything in this world" (*Since Cumorah,* 356).

But we need money, do we not? We need it to secure food, shelter, clothing, and much more. The question is, how much is enough? Brother Nibley answers the question in this way:

> We have enough when we have sufficient for our needs—which is very soon, we learn in
> 1 Timothy—"having food and raiment let us be therewith content" (1 Timothy 6:5–11). But . . . "they
> that will be rich fall into temptation," which means desires for things which they shouldn't have.
> This leads many people astray. . . . "Have you any money?" Sure, sufficient for our needs.
>
> "That's all right, but we need more."
>
> You don't; you don't need more than you need. More than enough is more than enough. . . .
> We are ready for the real work when we have sufficient for our needs. . . . If we get sidetracked on
> supplying our needs, then we are in real trouble. [*Approaching Zion,* 106–7]

Satan, trying to divert us from the Lord's work, tempts us to sell our lives and our loyalty for money, as Zeezrom did with Amulek in the Book of Mormon:

> Zeezrom[3] began to question Amulek, saying: Will ye answer me a few questions which I shall
> ask you? . . .
>
> And Amulek said unto him: Yea, if it be according to the Spirit of the Lord, which is in me; for
> I shall say nothing which is contrary to the Spirit of the Lord.
>
> And Zeezrom said unto him: Behold, here are six onties of silver, and all these will I give thee
> if thou wilt deny the existence of a Supreme Being.
>
> Now Amulek said: O thou child of hell, why tempt ye me? Knowest thou that the righteous
> yieldeth to no such temptations? Believest thou that there is no God? I say unto you, Nay, thou
> knowest that there is a God, but thou lovest that lucre more than him. [Alma 11:21–24; see also
> Acts 8:14–21]

---

3. Alma 11:6 identifies an "ezrom" as a unit of silver in Nephite trade, so the very name "Ze-ezrom" may indicate the man's association with money.

THE RESTORATION

A hand-colored woodcut from the Nuremberg Chronicle (1493) shows God's true messengers dressed in white and teaching the gospel. At the same time, a false messenger (the Antichrist), dressed in the borrowed robes of a Catholic cardinal, preaches a sermon whispered into his ear by Satan. The top of the picture shows the ultimate end of the false priest, who is kept from heaven by Michael the Archangel while three demons pull him down to hell.

Satan is the great counterfeiter, using his teachers to lead God's children astray. As President Joseph F. Smith said:

> By every possible means he seeks to darken the minds of men and then offers them falsehood and deception in the guise of truth. Satan is a skillful imitator, and as genuine gospel truth is given the world in ever-increasing abundance, so he spreads the counterfeit coin of false doctrine. . . . [As] "the father of lies" he has . . . become, through the ages of practice in his nefarious work, [such an adept] that were it possible he would deceive the very elect. [Ludlow, *Latter-day Prophets Speak,* 20–21]

Joseph Smith described the state of religious contention and division that existed before the restoration of the gospel:

> There was in the place where we lived an unusual excitement on the subject of religion. It commenced with the Methodists, but soon became general among all the sects in that region of country. Indeed, the whole district of country seemed affected by it, and great multitudes united themselves to the different religious parties, which created no small stir and division amongst the people, some crying, "Lo, here!" and others, "Lo, there!" Some were contending for the Methodist faith, some for the Presbyterian, and some for the Baptist. [Joseph Smith–History 1:5]

Coming of the Antichrist, by Michael Wolgemut, Wilhelm Pleydenwurff, and workshop. Hand-colored woodcut in the Nuremberg Chronicle, 1493.

Unable to resolve these scenes of confusion, young Joseph turned to the scriptures, where he found the key that would open this last dispensation of the gospel: "If any of you lack wisdom, let him ask of God, that giveth to all men liberally, and upbraideth not; and it shall be given him" (James 1:5).

Later, Joseph described his experience as he sought an answer in prayer:

> After I had retired to the place where I had previously designed to go, having looked around me, and finding myself alone, I kneeled down and began to offer up the desires of my heart to God. I had scarcely done so, when immediately I was seized upon by some power which entirely overcame me, and had such an astonishing influence over me as to bind my tongue so that I could not speak. Thick darkness gathered around me, and it seemed to me for a time as if I were doomed to sudden destruction.[1]
>
> But, exerting all my powers to call upon God to deliver me out of the power of this enemy which had seized upon me, and at the very moment when I was ready to sink into despair and abandon myself to destruction—not to an imaginary ruin, but to the power of some actual being from the unseen world, who had such marvelous power as I had never before felt in any being— just at this moment of great alarm, I saw a pillar of light exactly over my head, above the brightness of the sun, which descended gradually until it fell upon me.
>
> It no sooner appeared than I found myself delivered from the enemy which held me bound. When the light rested upon me I saw two Personages, whose brightness and glory defy all description, standing above me in the air. One of them spake unto me, calling me by name and said, pointing to the other—*This is My Beloved Son. Hear Him!* [Joseph Smith–History 1:15–17]

Joseph also described a typical reaction of others to his experience:

> I happened to be in company with one of the Methodist preachers, who was very active in the before mentioned religious excitement; and, conversing with him on the subject of religion, I took occasion to give him an account of the vision which I had had. I was greatly surprised at his behavior; he treated my communication not only lightly, but with great contempt, saying it was all of the devil, that there were no such things as visions or revelations in these days; *that all such things had ceased with the apostles, and that there would never be any more of them.* [Joseph Smith–History 1:21]

---

1. Compare Joseph's experience with those of Moses and the Savior, discussed earlier.

Nevertheless, the Prophet persisted, as instructed by the Lord's true messengers. The introduction to the Doctrine and Covenants tells us:

> In the course of time, Joseph Smith was enabled by divine assistance to translate and publish the Book of Mormon. In the meantime he and Oliver Cowdery were ordained to the Aaronic Priesthood by John the Baptist in May 1829 (see D&C 13), and soon thereafter they were also ordained to the Melchizedek Priesthood by the ancient Apostles Peter, James, and John (see D&C 27:12). Other ordinations followed in which priesthood keys were conferred by Moses, Elijah, Elias [see Joseph Smith Translation, Matthew 17:11–14], and many ancient prophets (see D&C 110; 128:18, 21). These ordinations were, in fact, a restoration of divine authority to man on the earth. On April 6, 1830, under heavenly direction, the Prophet Joseph Smith organized the Church, and thus the true Church of Jesus Christ is once again operative as an institution among men, with authority to teach the gospel and administer the ordinances of salvation.

Thus, Joseph and his successors also became true messengers, holding the keys of the kingdom of God. The same is true of the prophets and apostles today, whom we receive as servants of the Lord:

He that **RECEIVETH** my servants **RECEIVETH** me;

and he that **RECEIVETH** me **RECEIVETH** my Father;

and he that **RECEIVETH** my Father **RECEIVETH**

my Father's kingdom;

therefore all that my Father hath

shall be given unto him.

And this is according to the oath and covenant

which belongeth to the priesthood.

(DOCTRINE AND COVENANTS 84:36–39)

The First Vision, 1911. Stained glass in the Brigham City Third Ward meetinghouse, Brigham City, Utah.

From a skylight ("El Transparente") in the ceiling of the cathedral in Toledo, Spain, statues of saints and angels welcome visitors to the kingdom of heaven. Decorated with fantastic figures done in stucco, painting, bronze castings, and multiple colors of marble, the skylight is a masterpiece of Baroque art created 1729–1732 by Narciso Tomé and his four sons (two architects, one painter, and one sculptor).

"STAND IN HOLY PLACES"

The restoration of the gospel brought with it a new level of life and spirituality, lifting those who accepted it from the world of wickedness onto a higher plane. The Lord commanded in 1838, "Come up hither unto the land of my people, even Zion" (D&C 117:9).

> Behold, it is my will, that all they who call on my name, and worship me according to mine everlasting gospel, should gather together, and stand in holy places; . . . that the work of the gathering together of my saints may continue, that I may build them up unto my name upon holy places; for the time of harvest is come, and my word must needs be fulfilled. [D&C 101:22, 64]

During the Millennium, this higher state of existence will exist everywhere, not just in the stakes of Zion. President Joseph Fielding Smith explained:

> When our Savior comes, the earth will be changed to a terrestrial condition and will then be made the fit abode for terrestrial beings, and this condition will last until after the close of the millennium when the earth will die and be raised again in a resurrection to receive its glory as a celestial body, which is its final state. We are living in the great day of restoration. The Lord has declared that all things are to be restored to their primitive condition. Our Tenth Article of Faith says, "We believe . . . that Christ will reign personally upon the earth; and, that the earth will be renewed and receive its paradisiacal glory." Too many have the idea that this has reference to the celestialized earth, but this is not the case. It refers to the restored earth as it will be when Christ comes to reign [see Isaiah 65:17–25; D&C 101:23–31]. [*Doctrines of Salvation*, 1:84]

For the righteous, this higher state of existence will also exist in the spirit world. Alma taught:

> Now, concerning the state of the soul between death and the resurrection—Behold, it has been made known unto me by an angel, that the spirits of all men, as soon as they are departed

from this mortal body, yea, the spirits of all men, whether they be good or evil, are taken home to that God who gave them life. And then shall it come to pass, that the spirits of those who are righteous are received into a state of happiness, which is called paradise, a state of rest, a state of peace, where they shall rest from all their troubles and from all care, and sorrow. [Alma 40:11–12]

"THE SPIRITS IN PRISON"

A supernal event in Christ's ministry occurred during the time his crucified body lay in the tomb. This event, now largely forgotten by many Christian churches, is the Savior's visit to the spirit world as described in 1 Peter 3:18–19: "Christ . . . hath once suffered for sins, the just for the unjust, that he might bring us to God, being put to death in the flesh, but quickened by the Spirit: by which also he went and preached unto the spirits in prison." 1 Peter 4:6 gives us additional information, noting that the Savior preached "to them that are dead, that they might be judged according to men in the flesh, but live according to God in the spirit."

On October 3, 1918, President Joseph F. Smith pondered over these verses. As he did so, he received a vision of the redemption of the dead:

> The eyes of my understanding were opened, and the Spirit of the Lord rested upon me, and I saw the hosts of the dead, both small and great. And there were gathered together in one place an innumerable company of the spirits of the just, who had been faithful in the testimony of Jesus while they lived in mortality; and who had offered sacrifice in the similitude of the great sacrifice of the Son of God, and had suffered tribulation in their Redeemer's name. All these had departed the mortal life, firm in the hope of a glorious resurrection, through the grace of God the Father and his Only Begotten Son, Jesus Christ.
>
> I beheld that they were filled with joy and gladness, and were rejoicing together because the day of their deliverance was at hand. They were assembled awaiting the advent of the Son of God into the spirit world, to declare their redemption from the bands of death. . . .
>
> While this vast multitude waited and conversed, rejoicing in the hour of their deliverance from the chains of death, the Son of God appeared, declaring liberty to the captives who had been faithful; and there he preached to them the everlasting gospel, the doctrine of the resurrection and the redemption of mankind from the fall, and from individual sins on conditions of repentance. . . .

The Harrowing of Hell, *detail, by Duccio di Buoninsegna. Tempera on panel, 1308–1311.*

And the saints rejoiced in their redemption, and bowed the knee and acknowledged the Son of God as their Redeemer and Deliverer from death and the chains of hell. Their countenances shone, and the radiance from the presence of the Lord rested upon them, and they sang praises unto his holy name. [D&C 138:11–24]

Joseph Smith wrote:

Shall we not go on in so great a cause? Go forward and not backward. Courage, . . . and on, on to the victory! Let your hearts rejoice, and be exceedingly glad. Let the earth break forth into singing. Let the dead speak forth anthems of eternal praise to the King Immanuel, who hath ordained, before the world was, that which would enable us to redeem them out of their prison; for the prisoners shall go free. [D&C 128:22]

During the Middle Ages, the rescue of these souls was known as the "harrowing of hell," and it was the subject of numerous works of art. These paintings show Jesus conquering the demons and releasing the dead from their terrible bondage, with Adam and Eve the first to be pulled from torment. The Savior is nearly always depicted lifting the captives by the wrist; perhaps this signifies a firmer grip than just taking them by the hand (see Isaiah 22:23; Ezra 9:8).

UNITED IN FAITH
AND PRAYER

After the apostle Paul preached in the city of Iconium, the people of that city stoned him, then "drew him out of the city, supposing he had been dead" (Acts 14:19). What happened next, however, is particularly interesting: "Howbeit, as the disciples *stood round about him,* he rose up, and came into the city: and the next day he departed with Barnabas to Derbe" (Acts 14:20).

What did the disciples do that brought Paul back to health? The scriptures provide a possible answer: "Is any sick among you? let him call for the elders of the church; and let them pray over him" (James 5:14).

A very early apocryphal work, the Acts of John (written about A.D. 130), portrays Jesus and his apostles forming a circle to pray together before his arrest and trial:

> [Jesus] gathered all of us together and said: Before I am delivered up unto them let us sing an hymn to the Father, and so go forth to that which lieth before us. He bade us therefore make as it were a ring, holding one another's hands, and himself standing in the midst he said: Answer Amen unto me. He began, then, to sing [or recite] an hymn and to say: Glory be to thee, Father. And we, going about in a ring, answered him: Amen. [Acts of John 94, in James, *The New Testament Apocrypha,* 253; see Mark 14:26]

We see a similar practice among the Nephites:

> They did rejoice and *cry again with one voice,* saying: May the God of Abraham, and the God of Isaac, and the God of Jacob, protect this people in righteousness, so long as they shall call on the name of their God for protection. And it came to pass that they did break forth, *all as one,* in

singing, and praising their God for the great thing which he had done for them, in preserving them from falling into the hands of their enemies. [3 Nephi 4:30–31]

To be effective, however, such prayers had to follow certain requirements:

Have faith in God. . . . What things soever ye desire, when ye pray, believe that ye receive them, and ye shall have them. And when ye stand praying, forgive, if ye have ought against any: that your Father also which is in heaven may forgive you your trespasses. [Mark 11:22–25]

Therefore if thou bring thy gift to the altar, and there rememberest that thy brother hath ought against thee; leave there thy gift before the altar, and go thy way; first be reconciled to thy brother, and then come and offer thy gift. [Matthew 5:23–24]

Painting of a Christian woman wearing a veil during prayer, catacombs of Rome, about 199–217.

VEILING THE SACRED

n the thirteenth-century Byzantine church of Panagía Gorgoepíkoös, in Athens, Greece, is a veil that separates the altar holding the eucharist (the equivalent of the emblems of the sacrament) from the area in which the congregation assembles. The veil protects what is holy, just as we cover the sacrament table with a cloth, and it is decorated with *gammadia* (marks shaped like the Greek letter *gamma*), which have a symbolic meaning, possibly related to the blood on the doorposts during the original Passover: "The blood shall be to you for a token upon the houses where ye are" (Exodus 12:13). Anciently, many churches had such a veil, but in later churches it was replaced by a wooden barrier known as a *templon* or *iconostasis*. The doors in such barriers correspond with the "holy door" on which the pope ceremonially knocks three times with a mallet during jubilee years in Saint Peter's Basilica in Rome.

A veil is a symbol of separation and protection; it protects what is sacred from the common gaze. We see this in the story of Moses after he had finished speaking with the Lord:

> All the children of Israel came nigh: and he gave them in commandment all that the Lord had spoken with him in mount Sinai. And till Moses had done speaking with them, he put a veil on his face. But when Moses went in before the Lord to speak with him, he took the veil off, until he came out. And he came out, and spake unto the children of Israel that which he was commanded. And the children of Israel saw the face of Moses, that the skin of Moses' face shone: and Moses put the veil upon his face again, until he went in to speak with him. [Exodus 34:32–35]

Veil with gammadia in the thirteenth-century Byzantine church of Panagía Gorgoepíkoös, Athens, Greece.

CHASTITY AND MARRIAGE

Similar symbolism is used in the veil a bride wears during her wedding. This ancient practice signifies that the bride is not to be looked upon by the groom until the wedding vows have been exchanged. At that point, the groom lifts the bride's veil to kiss her, which is a symbolic precursor: "Adam *knew* Eve his wife; and she conceived" (Genesis 4:1).

This concept may also have something to do with why men and women are seated separately in synagogue and mosque, as such separation signifies the importance of chastity. Again, from the proclamation on the family: "God has commanded that the sacred powers of procreation are to be employed only between man and woman, lawfully wedded as husband and wife" (*Ensign*, November 2010).

And from the Bible: "Thou shalt not commit adultery" (Exodus 20:14).

Arnolfini Portrait, by Jan van Eyck. Panel painting, 1434. One of the great paintings of the Netherlandish Renaissance is this formal picture of a wealthy couple holding hands in the bedchamber of their Flemish home. The painting is filled with complex symbolism[1] and may be intended as a marriage contract, with the artist as witness, for his signature on the wall attests that "Jan van Eyck was here" (instead of the customary "Jan van Eyck made this"). The bride in the picture is not expecting; the fullness of the dress was simply a fashion of the time. But its green color indicates life, the hope of posterity, as does the placement of her hand. The groom raises his right hand in token of the marriage covenant, and he has removed the shoes from his feet, a reference to Exodus 3:5: "Put off thy shoes from off thy feet, for the place whereon thou standest is holy ground." Note the faithful dog at the bottom of the painting.

---

1. More information is available here: http://www.visual-arts-cork.com/famous-paintings/arnolfini-portrait.htm

Joseph Smith explained the eternal importance of the marriage covenant: "In the celestial glory there are three heavens or degrees; and in order to obtain the highest, a man must enter into this order of the priesthood [meaning the new and everlasting covenant of marriage]; and if he does not, he cannot obtain it. He may enter into the other, but that is the end of his kingdom; he cannot have an increase" (D&C 131:1–4).

CHRIST AND HIS PEOPLE

Ultimately, marriage symbolism has reference to the relationship between Christ and his people. As John said in his great revelation:

There came unto me one of the seven angels which had the seven vials full of the seven last plagues, and talked with me, saying, Come hither, *I will shew thee the bride,* the Lamb's wife. And he carried me away in the spirit to a great and high mountain, and shewed me that great city, the holy Jerusalem, descending out of heaven from God [being previously hidden], having the glory of God: and her light was like unto a stone most precious, even like a jasper stone, clear as crystal. [Revelation 21:9–11]

John watches as the New Jerusalem descends from heaven. Apocalypse Tapestry, by Jean Bondol and Nicholas Bataillie, between 1377 and 1380.

THE MOST HOLY PLACE

In the temple anciently, the veil separated the holy place from the *most* holy place, which contained the ark of the covenant:

> Thou shalt make a veil of blue, and purple, and scarlet, and fine twined linen of cunning work: with cherubims shall it be made: and thou shalt hang it upon four pillars of shittim wood overlaid with gold: their hooks shall be of gold, upon the four sockets of silver. And thou shalt hang up the veil under the taches [hooks or clasps], that thou mayest bring in thither within the veil the ark of the testimony: and *the veil shall divide unto you* between the holy place and the most holy. [Exodus 26:31–33]

At the Savior's crucifixion, the veil of the temple was torn asunder:

> Jesus, when he had cried again with a loud voice, yielded up the ghost. And, behold, the veil of the temple was rent in twain from the top to the bottom; and the earth did quake, and the rocks rent; and the graves were opened; and many bodies of the saints which slept arose, and came out of the graves after his resurrection, and went into the holy city, and appeared unto many. [Matthew 27:50–53]

Paul explained the significance of this event: "[We now have] boldness to enter into the holiest [place] by the blood of Jesus, by the new and living way, which he hath consecrated for us, through the veil, that is to say, his flesh" (Hebrews 10:19–20).

The Rending of the Veil, *by William Bell Scott. Watercolor heightened with gouache on paper, 1869.*

BUILDING THE KINGDOM

n the book of Revelation, John sees in vision an angel with a measuring instrument in his hand. The angel is measuring the New Jerusalem, the city of Zion, presumably so that John, knowing the dimensions of the city in heaven, will be able to help build it on earth (see image, p. 114).

> He that talked with me had a golden reed to measure the city, and the gates thereof, and the wall thereof. And the city lieth foursquare, and the length is as large as the breadth: and he measured the city with the reed, twelve thousand furlongs. The length and the breadth and the height of it are equal. And he measured the wall thereof, an hundred and forty and four cubits, according to the measure of a man, that is, of the angel. [Revelation 21:15–17]

If we are to build the city of Zion, we must use the tools the Lord has given us. These are represented in the scriptures in various ways. For example, Ezekiel saw an angel with a line of flax in his hand, that is, a length of string (see Ezekiel 40:2–4). Anyone who has put up a fence knows that a string tied between two posts is a horizontal guide that helps the builder keep the fence slats even and constant. The measuring reed, on the other hand, is the equivalent of a modern tape measure, which enables us to be exact in our construction.

In the art of the Middle Ages, the Creator is often depicted with a drafting compass. This tool was essential in the planning and building of the great Medieval cathedrals, so the artists naturally associated it with creation. If you recall your high school geometry class, you may remember that a compass is used to draw a circle. And the circle, of course, represents eternity. The Prophet Joseph Smith said, "I take my ring from my finger and liken it unto the mind of man—the immortal part,

The Heavenly Jerusalem *(detail), by Matthias Gerung. Illumination from the Ottheinrich Bible, folio 303v. Tempera on vellum, about 1530–1532. On the right, angels measure the celestial city while John looks on.*

because it has no beginning. Suppose you cut it in two; then it has a beginning and an end; but join it again, and it continues one eternal round."[1]

The circle is a common architectural element on the Salt Lake Temple and many other temples as well. Surely the architects who designed the temples did not use this element by chance; understanding its symbolic meaning, they purposely included it in various temple gates and walls. But often they put the circle inside a square, which traditionally refers to the earth in its fallen, temporal condition: "Even so will I gather mine elect from the four quarters of the earth, even as many as will believe in me, and hearken unto my voice" (D&C 33:6). Figure 6 in the book of Abraham's Facsimile No. 2 "represents this earth in its four quarters."

1. http://josephsmithpapers.org, History, 1838–1856, volume E-1 [1 July 1843–30 April 1844], 1974.

"Ici crie Dex ciel et terre, soleil et lune et toz elemenz" ("Here God creates heaven and earth, sun and moon and their elements"). *Codex Vindobonensis 2554, folio 1v, tempera on parchment, circa 1220–1230.* Medieval scholars believed that God created the universe using geometric principles, and that to study those principles was to seek and worship him.

When the circle and square are joined, they represent the eternal entering the temporal, which of course is what a temple is—a place where heaven and earth meet. And just as the American embassy in another country is considered to be American soil, so is a temple a bit of heaven on earth.

Because the symbol of a circle in a square represents the divine condescending to interact with the human, it can also represent a person who is filled with the Holy Ghost: "Know ye not that ye are the temple of God, and that the Spirit of God dwelleth in you?" (1 Corinthians 3:16). Furthermore, it has reference to our immortal spirits being born into our mortal bodies. But perhaps the circle in the square, as a symbol of the eternal entering the temporal, can have an even deeper meaning:

> In the beginning was the Word, and the Word was with God, and the Word was God. . . . And the Word was made flesh, and dwelt among us. [John 1:1, 14]
> Behold, I am Jesus Christ, whom the prophets testified shall come into the world. [3 Nephi 11:10]

Truly, "all things which have been given of God from the beginning of the world, unto man, are the typifying of [Christ]" (2 Nephi 11:4).

WHOM DO WE SERVE?

What else can we learn from the tools the Lord has given us? As we use these tools, we must remember that we are in the Savior's employ and not that of the world: "No servant can serve two masters: for either he will hate the one, and love the other; or else he will hold to the one, and despise the other. Ye cannot serve God and mammon" (Luke 16:13).

A page from the Bedford Book of Hours in the British Library depicts the construction of the Tower of Babel, with workmen using various tools (including compass and square) to plan and build their monument to human vanity: "Go to, let us build us a city and a tower, whose top may reach unto heaven; and let us make us a name, lest we be scattered abroad upon the face of the whole earth." Yet even as they work, the angels descend to destroy their efforts: "So the Lord scattered them abroad from thence upon the face of all the earth: and they left off to build the city" (Genesis 11:4, 8).

This account teaches us that "except the Lord build the house, they labour in vain that build it" (Psalm 127:1). So in our everyday lives, what is it we are building? Whom do we serve? *Why* do we serve? "A man's life consisteth not in the abundance of the things which he possesseth" (Luke 12:15). "What shall it profit a man, if he shall gain the whole world, and lose his own soul?"

Building the Tower of Babel. *Illumination from the Bedford Book of Hours, folio 17v. Tempera on parchment, about 1420.*

Jacob Blessing Ephraim and Manasseh, *by Benjamin West. Oil on canvas, 1768. See Genesis 48:8–20.*

(Mark 8:36). As we rightly direct our labors, our work will bear fruit, and the city that the angel measured in John's vision will someday become a reality:

> And I saw a new heaven and a new earth: for the first heaven and the first earth were passed away. . . . And I John saw the holy city, new Jerusalem, coming down from God out of heaven, prepared as a bride adorned for her husband. And I heard a great voice out of heaven saying, Behold, the tabernacle of God is with men, and he will dwell with them, and they shall be his people, and God himself shall be with them, and be their God. And God shall wipe away all tears from their eyes; and there shall be no more death, neither sorrow, nor crying, neither shall there be any more pain: for the former things are passed away. And he that sat upon the throne said, Behold, I make all things new. [Revelation 21:1–5]

CONSECRATION

The word usually translated as "consecrated" in the Bible comes from two Hebrew words whose literal meaning is "filled hand." We see an example of the use of "consecrated" in the book of Leviticus: "He that is the high priest among his brethren, upon whose head the anointing oil was poured, and *that is consecrated* to put on the garments, shall not uncover his head, nor rend his clothes" (Leviticus 21:10).

The footnote for this verse explains that the phrase "that is consecrated" means "whose hand is filled; i.e., who is equipped or authorized." The Hebrew words are *male'* and *yad. Male'* means "filled"; *yad* means "hand," which can be a symbol of strength or power: "Fear thou not; for I am with thee: be not dismayed; for I am thy God: I will strengthen thee; yea, I will help thee; yea, I will uphold thee with the right hand of my righteousness" (Isaiah 41:10; see also *Hymns,* 85, verse 3).

Hugh Nibley provided further insight: "[In ancient Israel] incense was often burned in special holders made in the form of a cupped hand, the 'golden spoons' of Exodus 25:29. . . . The 'filled hand' (the Hebrew letter *kaph* means 'palm') is the widespread sign of offering sacrifice" (*Temple and Cosmos,* 106).

Perhaps an *unfilled* hand, turned downward, could signify the giving of a blessing or the bestowing of authority: "The Lord said unto Moses, Take thee Joshua the son of Nun, a man in whom is the spirit, and *lay thine hand upon him;* and set him before Eleazar the priest, and before all the congregation; and give him a charge in their sight" (Numbers 27:18–19).

THE SACRED EMBRACE

Pompeo Batoni's painting of the prodigal son depicts the moment when the father embraces his wayward child after the son's repentant return:

> When [the prodigal son] came to himself, he said, How many hired servants of my father's have bread enough and to spare, and I perish with hunger! I will arise and go to my father, and will say unto him, Father, I have sinned against heaven, and before thee, and am no more worthy to be called thy son: make me as one of thy hired servants.
>
> And he arose, and came to his father. But when he was yet a great way off, his father saw him, and had compassion, and ran, and fell on his neck, and kissed him. And the son said unto him, Father, I have sinned against heaven, and in thy sight, and am no more worthy to be called thy son.
>
> But the father said to his servants, Bring forth the best robe, and put it on him; and put a ring on his hand, and shoes on his feet: and bring hither the fatted calf, and kill it; and let us eat, and be merry: for this my son was dead, and is alive again; he was lost, and is found. [Luke 15:17–24]

The painting is a tender, intimate portrait that brings to mind the words of Nephi: "O Lord, wilt thou encircle me around in the robe of thy righteousness!" (2 Nephi 4:33). "The Lord hath redeemed my soul from hell; I have beheld his glory, and I am encircled about eternally in the arms of his love" (2 Nephi 1:15). And Alma taught, "Behold, [God] sendeth an invitation unto all men, for the arms of mercy are extended towards them, and he saith: Repent, and I will receive you" (Alma 5:33).

The Return of the Prodigal
Son, *by Pompeo Batoni.
Oil on canvas, 1773.*

ELIJAH

We see echoes of this embrace elsewhere in the scriptures, where it is shown as literally bringing the dead back to life. For example, while the prophet Elijah was staying with the widow of Zarephath,

> the son of the woman . . . fell sick; and his sickness was so sore, that there was no breath left in him. . . .
>
> And he said unto her, Give me thy son. And he took him out of her bosom, and carried him up into a loft, where he abode, and laid him upon his own bed. And he cried unto the Lord, and said, O Lord my God, hast thou also brought evil upon the widow with whom I sojourn, by slaying her son?
>
> *And he stretched himself upon the child three times,* and cried unto the Lord, and said, O Lord my God, I pray thee, let this child's soul come into him again. And the Lord heard the voice of Elijah; and the soul of the child came into him again, and he revived.
>
> And Elijah took the child, and brought him down out of the chamber into the house, and delivered him unto his mother: and Elijah said, See, thy son liveth. And the woman said to Elijah, *Now by this I know that thou art a man of God,* and that the word of the Lord in thy mouth is truth. [1 Kings 17:17–24]

ELISHA

Elisha, who was Elijah's prophetic successor, had a similar experience with the son of a Shunammite woman:

> When Elisha was come into the house, behold, the child was dead, and laid upon his bed. He went in therefore, and shut the door . . . , and prayed unto the Lord. And he went up, and lay upon the child, and put his mouth upon his mouth,[1] and his eyes upon his eyes, and his hands upon his hands: and he stretched himself upon the child; and the flesh of the child waxed warm. [2 Kings 4:32–34]

---

1. Compare Genesis 2:7: "The Lord God formed man of the dust of the ground, and breathed into his nostrils the breath of life; and man became a living soul."

Elisha Raising the Son of the Shunammite, by Frederic Leighton. Oil on canvas, 1881.

PAUL

The apostle Paul used a healing embrace to bring life to a young man who had fallen and died:

Upon the first day of the week, when the disciples came together to break bread, Paul preached unto them, ready to depart on the morrow; and continued his speech until midnight. And there were many lights in the upper chamber, where they were gathered together. And there sat in a window a certain young man named Eutychus, being fallen into a deep sleep: and as Paul was long preaching, he sunk down with sleep, and fell down from the third loft, and was taken up dead. And Paul went down, and fell on him, and *embracing him* said, Trouble not yourselves; for his life is in him. . . . And they brought the young man alive, and were not a little comforted. [Acts 20:7–12]

JACOB

We see another sacred embrace in a story from the Old Testament in which Jacob is given a new name: *Israel*. On his way to be reconciled with his brother Esau, Jacob sent his servants ahead with a gift of many goats and camels. Then,

Jacob and the Angel, Doberan Minster in Mecklenburg, Germany. Painted and gilded sculpture, about 1368.

he rose up that night, and took his two wives, and his two womenservants, and his eleven sons, and passed over the ford Jabbok. And he took them, and sent them over the brook, and sent over that he had.

And Jacob was left alone; and there wrestled a man with him until the breaking of the day. . . .

And [the man] said, Let me go, for the day breaketh. And [Jacob] said, I will not let thee go, except thou bless me.

And [the man] said unto him, *What is thy name?* And he said, Jacob. And [the man] said, Thy name shall be called no more Jacob, but Israel: for *as a prince hast thou power with God and with men,* and hast prevailed.

And Jacob asked him, and said, *Tell me, I pray thee, thy name.* And [the man] said, Wherefore is it that thou dost ask after my name? And he blessed [Jacob] there. And Jacob called the name of the place Peniel: for [he said,] I have seen God face to face, and my life is preserved. [Genesis 32:22–30]

Truly, the knowledge received in this sacred embrace raises the recipient from death to life, bringing new understanding of the Lord's promise in the Word of Wisdom:

All saints who remember to keep and do these sayings, walking in obedience to the commandments, shall receive health in their navel and marrow to their bones; and shall find wisdom and great treasures of knowledge, even hidden treasures; and shall run and not be weary, and shall walk and not faint. And I, the Lord, give unto them a promise, that the destroying angel shall pass by them, as the children of Israel, and not slay them. Amen. [D&C 89:18–21]

THE FIVE WOUNDS OF CHRIST

A common theme in medieval art was the five wounds of Christ, traditionally the holes of the nails in the Savior's hands and feet and the cut of the spear through his side and into his heart. This theme of the five wounds has been celebrated in masses, rosaries, and works of art and literature. For example, John Lydgate of Bury (1370–1451), an English monk and a prolific poet, wrote the following verse, which, like many others of the time, compares Christ's wounds with wells of life-giving water:

At wells five, liquor I shall draw,
To wash the rust of my sins quickly,
I mean the wells of Christ's wounds five,
Whereby we claim of merciful pity.

(In Williams, *The Five Wounds of Jesus,* 23)

In the Middle Ages, the five wounds were symbolized in church decoration as a five-pointed star. This symbol is still used in temples today, including windows of the Nauvoo Illinois Temple.

During the construction of the Logan Utah Temple, a newspaper reported that the five-pointed star with an elongated bottom ray symbolized "the Star of the Morning," which is a title of the Lord (*Deseret Evening News,* August 20, 1880, 3; see Revelation 22:16). Again the elongated bottom ray pointing downward indicates that the Savior has descended from heaven to earth.

The Five Wounds of Christ, *by Sigmund Grimm. Woodcut, 1520.*

Traditionally, the five-pointed star is known as the Star of Bethlehem.

Other elements of temple worship are related to the number five: During the endowment we actually or symbolically visit five rooms, make five covenants, receive a charge composed of five elements, put on five articles of temple clothing, tie five bows on our clothing (symbols of connection), and witness five visits of heavenly messengers to our first parents and their posterity. Surely this is not the result of chance; all of these (and more) point to the Savior as the "well of living water" (D&C 63:23) and the "fount of every blessing" (*Hymns*, 1948, no. 70).

Five-pointed star on the Nauvoo Temple, by William Weeks. Original architectural drawing, 1840.

Five-pointed stars on the Nauvoo Illinois Temple.

JUDGMENT

n a painting of the Last Judgment, artist Hans Memling shows the resurrected dead being welcomed to heaven, where angels clothe the souls of the blessed in new robes before they enter the presence of the Lord. The painting brings to mind President Brigham Young's definition of the endowment:

> Your endowment is, to receive all those ordinances in the house of the Lord, which are necessary for you, after you have departed this life, to enable you to walk back to the presence of the Father, passing the angels who stand as sentinels, being enabled to give them the key words, the signs and tokens, pertaining to the holy Priesthood, and gain your eternal exaltation in spite of earth and hell. [*Discourses,* 416]

"THE KEEPER OF THE GATE"

Whoever (or, symbolically, whatever) these angels might be, the most important "angel" is, of course, the Lord himself. As Nephi said:

> O then, my beloved brethren, come unto the Lord, the Holy One. Remember that his paths are righteous. Behold, the way for man is narrow, but it lieth in a straight course before him, and the keeper of the gate is the Holy One of Israel; and he employeth no servant there; and there is none other way save it be by the gate; for he cannot be deceived, for the Lord God is his name. [2 Nephi 9:41]

And for whom will the Lord open the gate?

Whoso knocketh, to him will he open; and the wise, and the learned, and they that are rich, who are puffed up because of their learning, and their wisdom, and their riches—yea, they are they whom he despiseth; and save they shall cast these things away, and consider themselves fools before God, and come down in the depths of humility, he will not open unto them. But the things of the wise and the prudent shall be hid from them forever—yea, that happiness which is prepared for the saints. [2 Nephi 9:42–43]

The Last Judgment, *detail, by Hans Memling. Oil on panel, about 1470.*

We can learn much about the keeper of the gate from the experience of the brother of Jared:

It came to pass that [after] the brother of Jared had [made his request to the Lord], behold, the Lord stretched forth his hand. . . . And the veil was taken from off the eyes of the brother of Jared, and *he saw the finger of the Lord; and it was as the finger of a man, like unto flesh and blood*; and the brother of Jared fell down before the Lord, for he was struck with fear.

And the Lord saw that the brother of Jared had fallen to the earth; and the Lord said unto him: Arise, why hast thou fallen?

And he saith unto the Lord: I saw the finger of the Lord, and I feared lest he should smite me; for I knew not that the Lord had flesh and blood.

And the Lord said unto him: Because of thy faith thou hast seen that I shall take upon me flesh and blood; and never has man come before me with such exceeding faith as thou hast; for were it not so ye could not have seen my finger. Sawest thou more than this?

And he answered: Nay; Lord, show thyself unto me.

And the Lord said unto him: Believest thou the words which I shall speak?

And he answered: Yea, Lord, I know that thou speakest the truth, for thou art a God of truth, and canst not lie.

And when he had said these words, behold, the Lord showed himself unto him, and said: Because thou knowest these things ye are redeemed from the fall; *therefore ye are brought back into my presence;* therefore I show myself unto you. Behold, I am he who was prepared from the foundation of the world to redeem my people. Behold, I am Jesus Christ. I am the Father and the Son. In me shall all mankind have life, and that eternally, even they who shall believe on my name; and they shall become my sons and my daughters. [Ether 3:6–14]

"TO FAMILIARIZE HEAVEN AND EARTH"

President Brigham Young commented:

There is a mystery concerning the God I worship, which mystery will be removed when I come to a full knowledge of God. One of the greatest things Joseph Smith ever did was to familiarize heaven and earth and cause them to shake hands together and become familiar together. . . . When I meet the God I worship, I expect to [meet a] personage with whom I have been acquainted upon the same principle that I would to meet with my earthly father after going upon a journey and returning home. [Diary of Wilford Woodruff, January 27, 1860]

The hand of fellowship. Carving from the east tower of the Salt Lake Temple.

Ascension of Christ. *Ivory plaque, Milan or Rome, about 400.*

"WHILE THEY BEHELD, HE WAS TAKEN UP"

In the Middle Ages and even earlier, artists often created paintings or sculptures of people entering heaven. In many of these artworks, people do not simply float up to the sky. Rather, they are typically shown grasping the hand of God, which is extended through a cloud or curtain to pull them up to the celestial world. A wonderful early example is an ivory plaque carved in Milan or Rome in about the year 400. On display in the Bavarian National Museum in Munich, Germany, it depicts Jesus ascending to the Father after his resurrection.

On the left is the sepulchre in which the Savior's body was laid to rest after his crucifixion. A

Roman soldier, with his spear, guards the tomb, while one of the disciples mourns. The olive tree behind the sepulchre denotes the garden of Gethsemane, but it may also represent life growing out of death—in other words, the Resurrection. On the right we see two of the disciples overawed as the Savior ascends in glory, grasping his Father's hand: "While they beheld, he was taken up; and a cloud received him out of their sight" (Acts 1:9).

"COME, YE BLESSED"

The Savior's resurrection made our resurrection possible; there is not just one resurrection but many:

> As in Adam all die, even so in Christ shall all be made alive. But every man in his own order. [1 Corinthians 15:22–23]
>
> These are they who shall have part in the first resurrection. These are they who shall come forth in the resurrection of the just. [D&C 76:64–65]
>
> These are they who shall not be redeemed from the devil until the last resurrection, until the Lord, even Christ the Lamb, shall have finished his work. [D&C 76:85]

After the last resurrection, at the end of the Millennium, comes the Final Judgment, for, as Alma said, "The resurrection of the dead bringeth back men into the presence of God; and *thus they are restored into his presence, to be judged according to their works,* according to the law and justice" (Alma 42:23).

This idea was illustrated over and over during the Middle Ages, in paintings and sculptures on churches and cathedrals all over Europe, often in intricate detail. A magnificent example is found on a stone tympanum carved in about the year 1100 on the Church of Sainte-Foy at Conques, France. At the Savior's right hand are the righteous in heaven—Mary, Peter, and others. At the Savior's left hand (after four angels) are the wicked in hell, tormented by demons.[1]

The Savior's vivid description of the Final Judgment is the basis for many works of art:

> When the Son of man shall come in his glory, and all the holy angels with him, then shall he sit upon the throne of his glory: and before him shall be gathered all nations: and he shall separate

---

1. More images and information are available online: http://www.art-roman-conques.fr/english/index.htm.

The Last Judgment, *detail. Stone tympanum at the Church of Sainte-Foy, Conques, France, about 1100. Remnants of the original paint are still visible.*

Jesus enthroned in majesty, detail from The Last Judgment.

them one from another, as a shepherd divideth his sheep from the goats: and he shall set the sheep on his right hand, but the goats on the left.

Then shall the King say unto them on his right hand, Come, ye blessed of my Father, inherit the kingdom prepared for you from the foundation of the world: for I was an hungred, and ye gave me meat: I was thirsty, and ye gave me drink: I was a stranger, and ye took me in: naked, and ye clothed me: I was sick, and ye visited me: I was in prison, and ye came unto me. . . . Verily I say unto you, Inasmuch as ye have done it unto one of the least of these my brethren, ye have done it unto me.

Then shall he say also unto them on the left hand, Depart from me, ye cursed, into everlasting fire, prepared for the devil and his angels: for I was an hungred, and ye gave me no meat: I was thirsty, and ye gave me no drink: I was a stranger, and ye took me not in: naked, and ye clothed me not: sick, and in prison, and ye visited me not. . . . Verily I say unto you, Inasmuch as ye did it not to one of the least of these, ye did it not to me. And these shall go away into everlasting punishment: but the righteous into life eternal. [Matthew 25:31–46]

Greetings in Paradise, *by Giovanni di Paolo. Tempera and gold on canvas, transferred from wood, 1445.*

"THAT SAME SOCIALITY"

After finishing a temple session, you may sit quietly in the celestial room, thinking about what you have just experienced. Looking about, you see elegant furnishings, soaring windows, sparkling chandeliers, all joining to lift your mind from earth to heaven. But there is also something infinitely more important in that room than its beautiful furnishings: The room is filled with people—often with family and friends.

Describing a vision of the celestial world, the Prophet Joseph Smith wrote, "I beheld the celestial kingdom of God, and the glory thereof. . . . I saw Father Adam and Abraham; and *my father and my mother; my brother Alvin,* that has long since slept" (D&C 137:1–5).

The Prophet promised, "That same sociality which exists among us here will exist among us there, only it will be coupled with eternal glory, which glory we do not now enjoy" (D&C 130:2). A poem by Joseph L. Townsend published in the *Juvenile Instructor* on October 15, 1879, describes what it might be like to meet in that holy place:

> *O, what songs of the heart*
> *We shall sing all the day,*
> *When again we assemble at home;*
> *When we meet, ne'er to part,*
> *With the blest o'er the way,*
> *There no more from our loved ones to roam! . . .*
>
> *O, what songs we shall sing,*
> *As, with angels of light,*
> *In triumphant procession we move,*

While our harps sweetly ring[1]
Through the city so bright,
When we meet with our Savior above. . . .

O, what songs we'll employ!
O, what welcomes we'll hear!
While our transports of love are complete;
As the heart swells with joy
In embraces most dear,
When our heavenly parents we meet!
[See Hymns, *286]*

Describing his great vision of the celestial world, John the Revelator wrote:

One of the elders answered, saying unto me, What are these which are arrayed in white robes? and whence came they? And I said unto him, Sir, thou knowest. And he said to me, These are they which came out of great tribulation, and have washed their robes, and made them white in the blood of the Lamb. Therefore are they before the throne of God, and serve him day and night in his temple: and he that sitteth on the throne shall dwell among them. They shall hunger no more, neither thirst any more; neither shall the sun light on them, nor any heat. For the Lamb which is in the midst of the throne shall feed them, and shall lead them unto living fountains of waters: and God shall wipe away all tears from their eyes. [Revelation 7:13–17]

And the apostle Paul wrote, "Eye hath not seen, nor ear heard, neither have entered into the heart of man, the things which God hath prepared for them that love him" (1 Corinthians 2:9).

The Lord described those who will inherit the celestial glory: "Then shall they be gods, because they have no end; therefore shall they be from everlasting to everlasting, because they continue; then shall they be above all, because all things are subject unto them. Then shall they be gods, because they have all power, and the angels are subject unto them" (D&C 132:20).

At this point we have come full circle. We can now understand why, in the beginning, we were shown so carefully how the world was made, and why, in the end, we were given the tools of creation and taught their proper use. We can now understand the real purpose and importance of the *family:*

---

1. "Praise ye the Lord. . . . Praise him with the psaltery and harp" (Psalm 150:1, 3).

John on the Isle of Patmos. *Illumination from the Très riches heures du duc de Berry, folio 17r.*
Tempera on vellum, between 1411 and 1416.

Little Garden of Paradise, *by an artist known as the Upper Rhenish Master. Tempera on wood, about 1410–1420. Here, family and friends enjoy being together in the celestial world. Amid trees and flowers, they read, converse, play music, and taste the sweet fruits and refreshing water of heaven. The murals in the celestial room of the Idaho Falls Temple depict similar scenes.*[2]

Abraham received promises concerning his seed, and of the fruit of his loins . . . which were to continue so long as they were in the world; and as touching Abraham and his seed, out of the world they should continue; both *in the world and out of the world* should they continue as innumerable as the stars; or, if ye were to count the sand upon the seashore ye could not number them. This promise is yours also, because ye are of Abraham, and the promise was made unto Abraham; and by this law is the continuation of the works of my Father, wherein he glorifieth himself. [D&C 132:30–31]

We now understand, in a small way, what it means to take part in God's great work, "to bring to pass the immortality and eternal life of man" (Moses 1:39), so that, like our Progenitors, we may someday say to those who are with us, "See, yonder is matter unorganized" (Nibley, *Old Testament and Related Studies*, 76).

---

2. See examples at http://ldspioneerarchitecture.blogspot.com/2014/08/idaho-falls-temple.html.

THE MESSAGE OF
THE TEMPLE

On Christmas Eve, 1513, the Italian monk Giovanni Giocondo wrote a letter to his friend the Countess Allagia Aldobrandeschi. In the letter, he beseeched her to look for the meaning behind the trials of mortality, the purpose behind her problems, just as we do when we look for the meaning behind temple symbols. His message is timeless and true. In its essence, it echoes the message of the temple:

There is nothing I can give you which you have not got; but there is much, very much, that, while I cannot give it, you can take. No heaven can come to us unless our hearts find rest in it today. Take heaven! No peace lies in the future which is not hidden in this present little instant. Take peace! The gloom of the world is but a shadow. Behind it, yet within our reach, is joy. There is radiance and glory in the darkness, could we but see; and to see, we have only to look. . . .

Life is so generous a giver, but we, judging its gifts by their covering, cast them away as ugly or heavy or hard. Remove the covering, and you will find beneath it a living splendour, woven of love, by wisdom, with power. Welcome it, grasp it, and you touch the angel's hand that brings it to you. Everything we call a trial, a sorrow, or a duty: believe me, that angel's hand is there; the gift is there, and the wonder of an over-shadowing Presence. Our joys, too: be not content with them as joys; they too conceal diviner gifts.

Life is so full of meaning and of purpose, so full of beauty beneath its covering, that you will find that earth but cloaks your heaven. Courage, then, to claim it: that is all! But courage you have; and the knowledge that we are pilgrims together, wending through unknown country, home.

Helping us to comprehend our eternal journey, the endowment embodies what are called the mysteries of godliness (see 1 Timothy 3:16; D&C 19:10)—those things that will enable us to understand the expression of the Savior made just before his betrayal: "This is life eternal, that they

Christ the Omnipotent, holding an ornately decorated gospel book. Icon at Hilandar Monastery on Mount Athos in northern Greece, about 1260. "A book of remembrance was written . . . for them that feared the Lord, and that thought upon his name. And they shall be mine, saith the Lord of hosts, in that day when I make up my jewels" (Malachi 3:16–17).

might know thee, the only true God, and Jesus Christ, whom thou hast sent" (John 17:3). This knowledge is not intellectual but *experiential*, an actual reuniting with our heavenly family.

Joseph Smith exulted:

> Let the mountains shout for joy, and all ye valleys cry aloud; and all ye seas and dry lands tell the wonders of your Eternal King! And ye rivers, and brooks, and rills, flow down with gladness. Let the woods and all the trees of the field praise the Lord; and ye solid rocks weep for joy! And let the sun, moon, and the morning stars sing together, and let all the sons of God shout for joy! And let the eternal creations declare his name forever and ever! And again I say, how glorious is the voice we hear from heaven, proclaiming in our ears, glory, and salvation, and honor, and immortality, and eternal life; kingdoms, principalities, and powers! . . .

> Let us, therefore, as a church and a people, and as Latter-day Saints, offer unto the Lord an offering in righteousness; and let us present in his holy temple, when it is finished, a book containing the records of our dead, which shall be worthy of all acceptation. [D&C 128:23–24]

The Pilgrim of the World on His Journey, *by Thomas Cole. Oil on canvas, about 1847.*

THE TEMPLE AND MODERN CULTURE

Unfortunately, a great deal of nonsense has been written about the temple, especially online. Critical bloggers are quick to point out what they see as indications of corporate oppression, subjugation of women, and so on. Focused on their own ideas, they misunderstand the teachings of the Lord's house, which need to be considered on their own terms rather than judged by our limited sensibilities.

The celestial world has its own culture, which is not the same as ours. And why should it be? Why should we *want* it to be? If you were to visit Paris, would you expect everyone to speak English? To think the way you do? To capitulate to your notions of how things should be? Rather than sampling French cuisine in a sidewalk cafe, would you seek out the nearest McDonald's? Rather than exploring the sights along the Seine, would you hurry back to the bland familiarity of your hotel? Or would you try to learn something new, to *experience* something new, to expand your horizons beyond your current, limited understanding? The great Christian apologist and medievalist C. S. Lewis wrote:

> There are, I know, those who prefer not to go beyond the impression, however accidental, which an *old work* [like the endowment] makes on a mind that brings to it a purely modern sensibility and modern conceptions; just as there are travellers who carry their resolute Englishry with them all over the Continent, mix only with other English tourists, enjoy all they see for its "quaintness," and have no wish to realise what those ways of life, those churches, those vineyards, mean to the natives. They have their reward. [*The Discarded Image,* ix–x]

The temple has much to teach us but only if we are willing to learn.

President Brigham Young noted:

> *Let us not narrow ourselves up;* for the world, with all its variety of useful information and its rich hoard of hidden treasure, is before us; and eternity, with all its sparkling intelligence, lofty aspirations, and unspeakable glories, is before us, and ready to aid us in the scale of advancement and every useful improvement. [In *Journal of Discourses,* 8:9]

Nowhere is that more true than in the temple, which has rightly been called the Lord's university (see for example, Porter, "Come to the Temple"). But to really understand the temple, we need to understand more about everything, for as Hugh Nibley says, "There is no part of our civilization which doesn't have its rise in the temple" (*Temple and Cosmos,* 25).

That may be why the Lord expects us to learn "of things both in heaven and in the earth, and under the earth; things which have been, things which are, things which must shortly come to pass; things which are at home, things which are abroad; the wars and the perplexities of the nations, and the judgments which are on the land; and a knowledge also of countries and of kingdoms" (D&C 88:79).

If you have learned a foreign language, you have probably found that you now better understand the grammar of your native tongue. If you have visited the Lake District in England, you probably better appreciate the poetry of Wordsworth. Any time we are able to compare one thing with another, we better understand them both, so the more we know, the more we *can* know. Thus, even though we have not directly discussed the teachings of the temple here, we *have* discussed scripture passages and works of art that can be *related* to the temple. I hope doing so has helped you better understand the meaning of the things we learn in the Lord's house.

Ultimately, our understanding depends on actually *going* to the Lord's house. We cannot get that understanding from others or give it *to* others. Elder John A. Widtsoe noted:

> One man may explain or show a symbol to another, and this is a common, everyday practice, but no man can reveal to another the sublime, deep inner meaning of those symbols presented in the House of the Lord, for it is an individual matter, and every man must seek and obtain it for himself, and that alone, with God's help only. Nor can one acquire this knowledge outside the House of the Lord, for there we must go to commune with him about these vital things. . . .

No man, however intellectual, can know these things, but by the revelations of God, and that in temples only. [*Power from on High*, 48–49]

Even then, we need to keep in mind the warning from Elder Gerald N. Lund: "[We must] fit the interpretation of any symbol into the overall scheme of gospel knowledge. No matter how clever, or how logical, or how ingenious our interpretation of a particular symbol may be, if it contradicts what is revealed in other places, we can assume it is wrong" ("Understanding Scriptural Symbols," 24).

That is why we should improve our knowledge by studying the best information available, particularly the scriptures, for the more we learn, the better equipped we will be to avoid error and the better we will understand those revelations the Lord is willing to give us. The Lord commanded the School of the Prophets, which met in the Kirtland Temple, "Seek ye diligently and teach one another words of wisdom; yea, *seek ye out of the best books words of wisdom; seek learning, even by study and also by faith*," (D&C 88:118). Following are a few suggestions for further reading:

Brown, Matthew. *The Gate of Heaven*. American Fork, Utah: Covenant Communications, 1999.

Campbell, Beverly. *Eve and the Choice Made in Eden*. Salt Lake City: Bookcraft, 2003.

Gaskill, Alonzo L. *Sacred Symbols: Finding Meaning in Rites, Rituals, and Ordinances*. Springville, Utah: Bonneville Books, 2011.

Nibley, Hugh. *Mormonism and Early Christianity*. Edited by Todd M. Compton and Stephen D. Ricks. Salt Lake City and Provo: Deseret Book and the Foundation for Ancient Research and Mormon Studies, 1987.

Nibley, Hugh. *Temple and Cosmos*. Edited by Don E. Norton. Salt Lake City and Provo: Deseret Book and the Foundation for Ancient Research and Mormon Studies, 1992.

Talmage, James E. *The House of the Lord*. Salt Lake City: Deseret Book, 1968.

Ulrich, Wendy. *The Temple Experience: Our Journey toward Holiness*. American Fork, Utah: Covenant Communications, 2012.

SOURCES

Boyer, Paul S., et al. *The Enduring Vision: A History of the American People.* 8th ed. 2 vols. Stamford: Cengage Learning, 2015.

Calvin, John. *Institutes of Christian Religion.* Translated by Henry Beveridge. Grand Rapids: Christian Classics Ethereal Library, 2002.

Challoner, Richard. *Think Well On't; or, Reflections on the Great Truths of the Christian Religion.* Manchester, England: T. Haydock, 1801.

Cyril of Jerusalem. *Catechetical Lectures.* Translated by Edwin Hamilton Gifford. In *Nicene and Post-Nicene Fathers,* second series (14 vols.), vol. 7. Edited by Philip Schaff and Henry Wace. Buffalo: Christian Literature Publishing Co., 1894.

Davies, Brian. *The Thought of Thomas Aquinas.* Oxford: Clarendon Press, 1993.

Deseret Evening News, August 20, 1880.

Durandus, William. *The Symbolism of Churches and Church Ornaments.* London: Gibbings & Co., 1906.

Holland, Jeffrey R. "The Inconvenient Messiah." *Ensign,* February 1984.

———. "The Ministry of Angels." *Ensign,* November 2008.

Hunter, Milton R. *The Gospel through the Ages.* Salt Lake City: Stevens and Wallis, 1945.

Hymns. Salt Lake City: The Church of Jesus Christ of Latter-day Saints, 1948.

Hymns of The Church of Jesus Christ of Latter-day Saints. Salt Lake City: The Church of Jesus Christ of Latter-day Saints, 1985.

James, M. R. *The New Testament Apocrypha.* Oxford: Clarendon Press, 2004.

Jessee, Dean C. "'Walls, Gates and Screeking Iron Doors': The Prison Experience of Mormon Leaders in Missouri, 1838–1839," in Davis Bitton and Maureen Ursenbach Beecher, *New Views of Mormon History: A Collection of Essays in Honor of Leonard J. Arrington.* Salt Lake City: University of Utah Press, 1987.

Journal of Discourses. 26 vols. Liverpool: F. D. and S. W. Richards, 1854.

Lewis, C. S. *The Discarded Image.* Cambridge: Cambridge University Press, 1995.

Lightbown, Ronald. *Carlo Crivelli.* New Haven, Conn.: Yale University Press, 2003.

Lowrie, Walter. *Art in the Early Church.* New York: W. W. Norton & Co., 1969.

Ludlow, Daniel H. *Latter-day Prophets Speak.* Salt Lake City: Bookcraft, 1948.

Lund, Gerald N. "Understanding Scriptural Symbols." *Ensign,* October 1986.

Maxwell, Neal A. "The Disciple-Scholar," in *On Becoming a Disciple-Scholar.* Edited by Henry B. Eyring. Salt Lake City: Bookcraft, 1995.

———. *Sermons Not Spoken.* Salt Lake City: Deseret Book, 2009.

Milton, John. *Paradise Lost.* Edited by Gordon Teskey. New York: W. W. Norton & Co., 2004.

Montgomery, James. *The Poetical Works of James Montgomery.* 5 vols. Boston: Little, Brown and Co., 1860.

Nelson, Russell M. "Personal Preparation for Temple Blessings." *Ensign,* May 2001.

Nibley, Hugh. *Ancient Documents and the Pearl of Great Price.* Edited by Robert Smith and Robert Smythe. Salt Lake City: Deseret Book, 1986.

————. *Approaching Zion.* Edited by Don E. Norton. Salt Lake City and Provo: Deseret Book and the Foundation for Ancient Research and Mormon Studies, 1989.

————. *The Message of the Joseph Smith Papyri.* Edited by John Gee and Michael D. Rhodes. Salt Lake City and Provo: Deseret Book and the Foundation for Ancient Research and Mormon Studies, 2005.

————. *Mormonism and Early Christianity.* Edited by Todd M. Compton and Stephen D. Ricks. Salt Lake City and Provo: Deseret Book and the Foundation for Ancient Research and Mormon Studies, 1987.

————. *Old Testament and Related Studies.* Edited by John W. Welch, Gary P. Gillum, and Don E. Norton. Salt Lake City and Provo: Deseret Book and the Foundation for Ancient Research and Mormon Studies, 1986.

————. *Since Cumorah.* Salt Lake City: Deseret Book, 1976.

————. *Temple and Cosmos.* Edited by Don E. Norton. Salt Lake City and Provo: Deseret Book and the Foundation for Ancient Research and Mormon Studies, 1992.

Noble, Louis Legrand. *The Life and Works of Thomas Cole.* Edited by Elliot S. Vesell. Hensonville, N.Y.: Black Dome Press, 1997.

Nyman, Monte S., and Charles D. Tate Jr., eds. *Alma: The Testimony of the Word.* Salt Lake City: Deseret Book, 1992.

Oaks, Dallin H. "Apostasy and Restoration." *Ensign,* May 1995.

Ogden, D. Kelly, Jared W. Ludlow, and Kerry Muhlestein, eds. *The Gospel of Jesus Christ in the Old Testament.* Provo and Salt Lake City: BYU Religious Studies Center and Deseret Book, 2009.

Oliver, George. *Historical Landmarks.* 2 vols. New York: John W. Leonard and Co., 1855.

Packer, Boyd K. "The Holy Temple." *Ensign,* February 1995.

Porter, L. Aldin. "Come to the Temple." *New Era,* October 2004.

Pratt, Parley P. *Key to the Science of Theology.* Salt Lake City: Deseret Book, 1948.

Smith, Joseph. *History of The Church of Jesus Christ of Latter-day Saints.* 2d ed. rev. Edited by B. H. Roberts. 7 vols. Salt Lake City: Deseret Book, 1991.

————.*Joseph Smith.* Teachings of Presidents of the Church series. Salt Lake City: The Church of Jesus Christ of Latter-day Saints, 2007.

————. "The King Follett Sermon." *Ensign,* April 1971.

————. Undated discourse, in "Extracts from William Clayton's Private Book," 7–8. *Journals of L. John Nuttall, 1857–1904.* L. Tom Perry Special Collections, Brigham Young University.

Smith, Joseph Fielding. *Doctrines of Salvation.* 3 vols. Salt Lake City: Bookcraft, 1954.

Snow, Eliza R. *Poems, Religious, Historical, and Political.* 2 vols. Liverpool: F. D. Richards, 1856; Salt Lake City: Latter-day Saints' Printing and Publishing Establishment, 1877.

Tertullian. *De Orationes.* Translated by S. Thelwall. In *Ante-Nicene Fathers* (10 vols.), vol. 3. Edited by Alexander Roberts, James Donaldson, and A. Cleveland Coxe. Buffalo: Christian Literature Publishing Co., 1885.

Townsend, Joseph L. "Songs of the Heart." *Juvenile Instructor,* October 15, 1879, 240.

Uchtdorf, Dieter F. "The Reflection in the Water." *Church News,* November 1, 2009.

Walton, John H. *Ancient Near Eastern Thought and the Old Testament.* Grand Rapids: Baker Academic, 2006.

Welch, John W. "The Good Samaritan: Forgotten Symbols." *Ensign,* February 2007.

Widtsoe, John A. *In a Sunlit Land: The Autobiography of John A. Widtsoe.* Salt Lake City: Deseret News, 1952.

————. *Power from on High.* Salt Lake City: Genealogical Society, 1937.

————. "Temple Worship." *Utah Genealogical and Historical Magazine,* April 1921.

Wilcox, S. Michael. *House of Glory: Finding Personal Meaning in the Temple.* Salt Lake City: Deseret Book, 1995.

Williams, David H. *The Five Wounds of Jesus.* Leominster, Herefordshire: Gracewing, 2004.

Woodruff, Wilford. Diary of Wilford Woodruff, January 27, 1860. Church History Library, The Church of Jesus Christ of Latter-day Saints, Salt Lake City, Utah.

Young, Brigham. *Discourses of Brigham Young.* Selected by John A. Widtsoe. Salt Lake City: Deseret Book, 1941.

IMAGE CREDITS